"The Dalai Lamas left their imprints on sacred landscape through centuries enlightenment wisdom in Tibet and throughout neighboring kingdoms. As architects inspired b monastic castles and retreated to power spots amidst soaring mountain belonging and connection to the realm of the divine, this spirit of place, is As this most beautiful of books reveals, the Dalai Lamas continue to teach ι of thinking, other ways of being, other ways of orienting ourselves in soc This idea, the quintessential expression of a perfect mandala world, can on

—Wade Davis, Explorer-in-Residence, National Geographic Society

GW01451416

"In Tibet, it is said, 'The sky is Buddhist and the land is Buddhist.' The presence of the Buddhist culture is thus felt not only in the many monasteries, philosophical colleges, and hermitages found everywhere on the Roof of the World, but also on hillsides covered with prayer flags and rocks carved with mantras. In such a world, the spiritual presence of the various incarnations of the Dalaï-lama has been a constant source of inspiration for many generations of Tibetans since the 14th century. In his beautiful book, Glenn Mullin, who has been close to the Dalaï-lamas' teachings, life stories, and blessings for the greater part of his life, shares with us a vision of a world that is deeply inspiring and poignant, as Tibet struggles to retain its spiritual and cultural identity."

— Matthieu Ricard, Buddhist monk, photographer, and author of *Happiness: A Guide to Developing Life's Most Important Skill*, *Tibet: An Inner Journey*, and *The Quantum and the Lotus*

"In Tibetan Buddhism, *khorra* (or, pilgrimage) to sacred sites and power places is considered to be spiritually healing and transformative. Today perhaps no one is better suited to lead us on khorra to the sacred sites of Tibet's Dalai Lamas than renowned tibetologist, Dalai Lama historian, and translator, Glenn Mullin. Accompanied by pristine photographs of places and people along the route, Mullin's commentary guides us wisely, and well."

—Jan Willis, author of *Dreaming Me: Black, Baptist and Buddhist—One Woman's Spiritual Journey*

"As this wonderfully illustrated book takes the reader on a journey to the magnificent sacred sites of central Tibet, its narrative sheds light on the history and methods of Buddhist pilgrimage practices. Through his engaging narrative, which weaves together historical facts, passages from Buddhist texts, writings of Dalai Lamas, and his own personal experiences, Glenn Mullin keeps the reader interested and edified."

—Vesna A. Wallace, Professor of Buddhist Studies, University of California, Santa Barbara

"Glenn Mullin is the consummate expert on the Dalai Lama and Tibetan/Buddhist culture. Everything Glenn writes or speaks about shimmers, captivates, and educates. This book is no exception."

—Lloyd Nick, Director, Oglethorpe University Museum of Art, Atlanta, GA

"A gorgeous book, full of extraordinary information."

—Joan Halifax, Buddhist teacher, anthropologist, and author of *Being with Dying*

"Having only experienced the Dalai Lama and Tibetan Buddhism in the West, I was missing a deeper experience. I have always hoped to be able to gain that experience and I now have begun through this remarkable book of photography and history. Thank you, Glen Mullin, for this most enlightening gift."

—Jun Po Denis Kelly Roshi, Zen Master and Abbot, Hollow Bones Sangha

THE
SACRED SITES
OF THE DALAI LAMAS

GLENN H. MULLIN

PHOTOGRAPHY BY:

GERRY CROCE / STEVE DANCZ / ROB DEMING

MICHAEL WIESE / WILLIAM P. WOOD JR.

EDITED BY:

DONALD McCREA

DIVINE
ARTS

To my sister & my friend. Things make much more sense with you around! I'm in awe of you, always. Lae you beyond words Sis!

Clae xx

2012

Published by DIVINE ARTS
DivineArtsMedia.com

An imprint of Michael Wiese Productions
12400 Ventura Blvd. #1111
Studio City, CA 91604
(818) 379-8799, (818) 986-3408 (FAX)

Cover design: Johnny Ink. www.johnnyink.com
Book Layout: William Morosi
Printed by SC (Sang Choy) International H.K. Limited

Printed in Hong Kong
Copyright 2011 by Glenn H. Mullin

Library of Congress Cataloging-in-Publication Data

Mullin, Glenn H.
The sacred sites of the Dalai Lamas / Glenn H. Mullin.
    p. cm.
ISBN 978-1-61125-006-0 (pbk.)
1. Buddhist pilgrims and pilgrimages--Tibet Region. 2. Dalai lamas. 3. Sacred space--Tibet Region. I. Title.
BQ6450.C62T5355 2011
294.3'4351--dc23
                    2011017823

CONTENTS

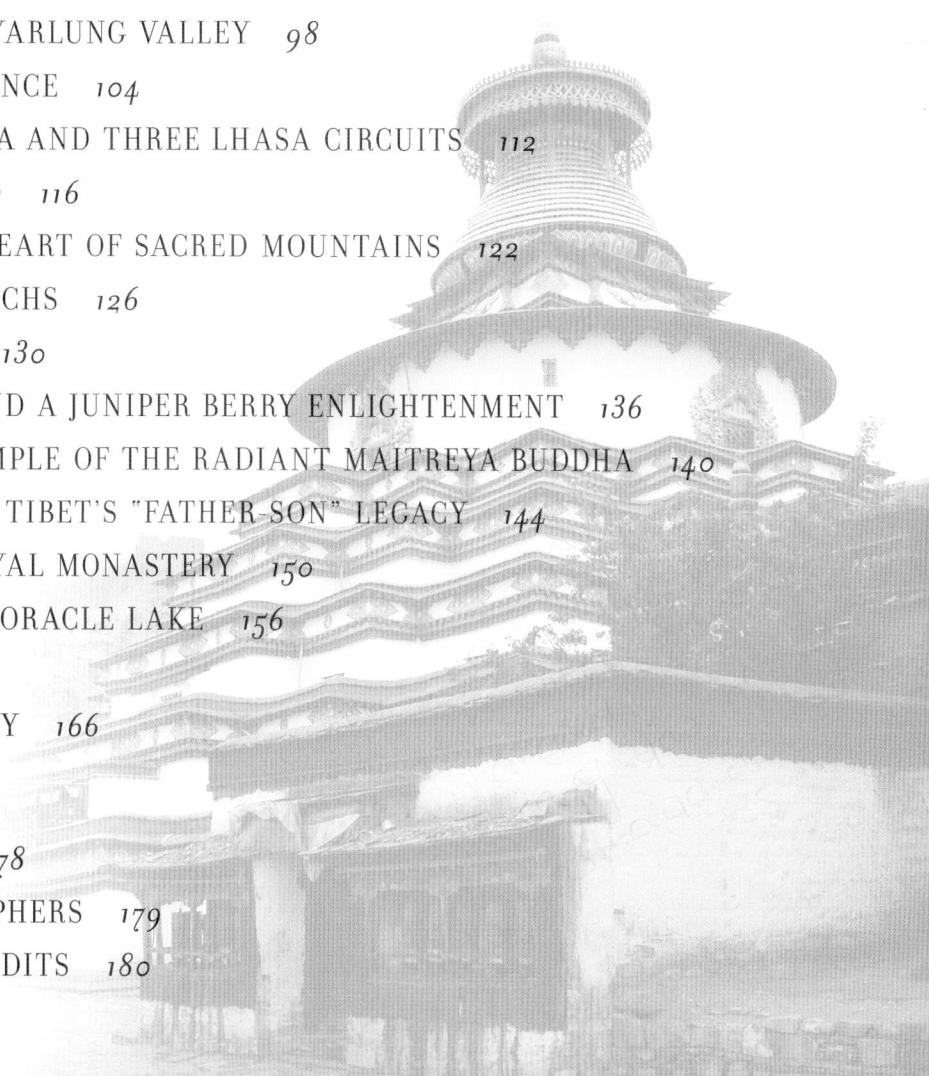

A MILLION SUNBEAMS DANCE FROM BEHIND GOLDEN MOUNTAINS;

They pervade and illuminate our world.

Yet more brilliant are the dazzling forms of enlightenment,

Radiant with the marks and signs of perfection.

■ FROM *Crushing All Negative Forces to Dust*

The First Dalai Lama, Gyalwa Gendun Druppa

1391-1475

THE IMAGES

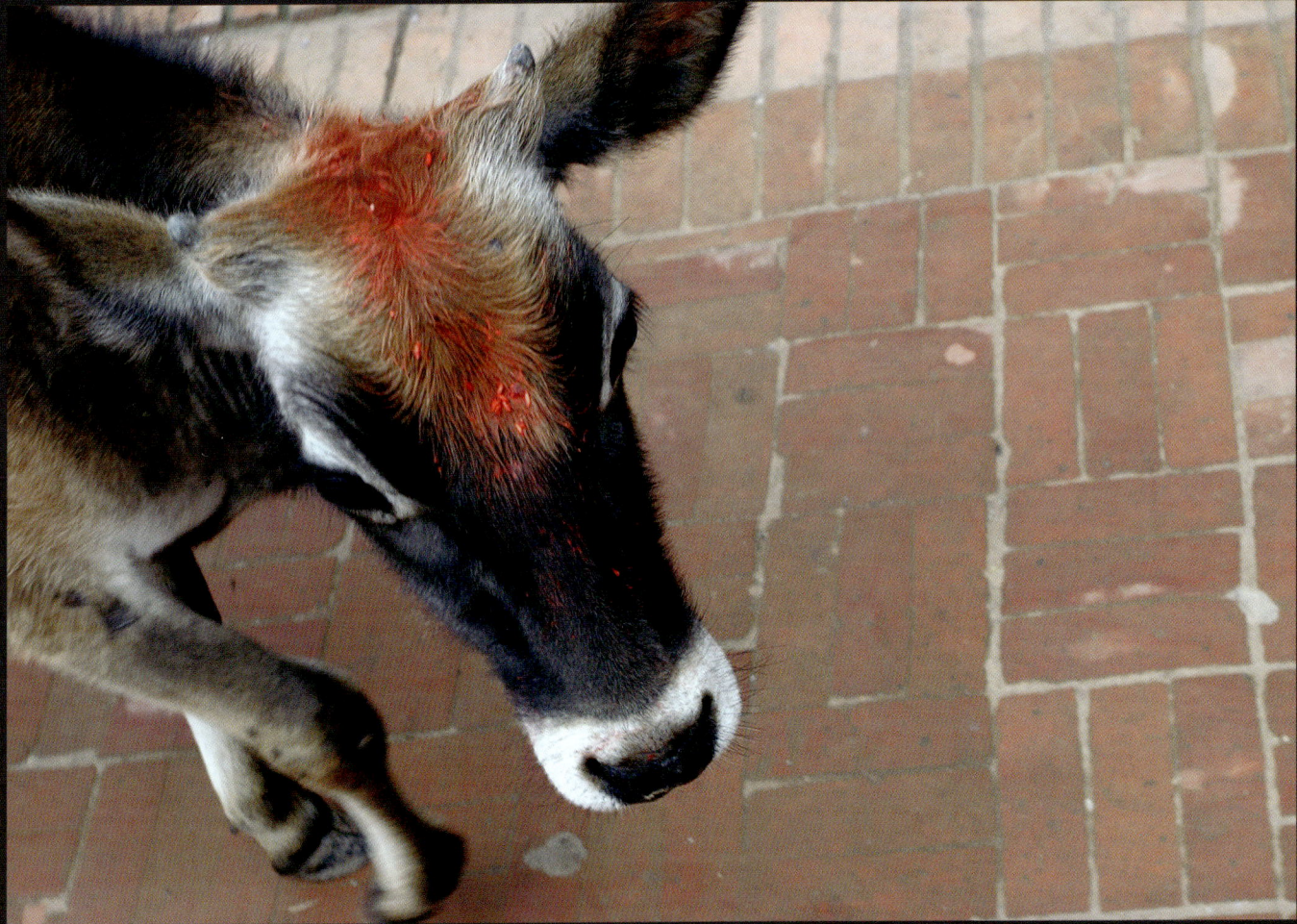

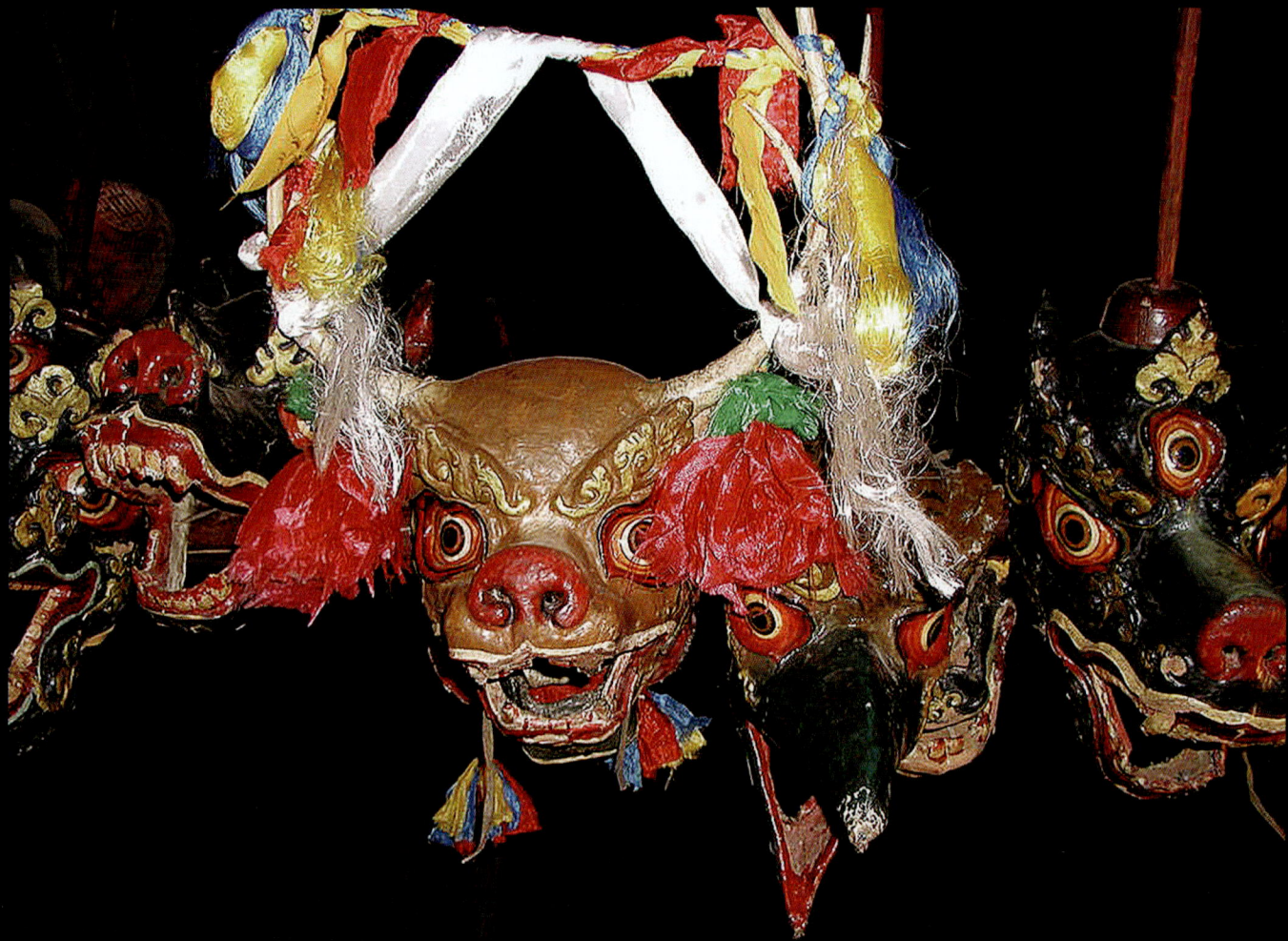

T

THE DALAI LAMAS

LTHOUGH SEVERAL OF THE FOURTEEN DALAI LAMA INCARNATIONS were born in remote areas, and two of them took birth outside of Tibet (the Fourth and Fourteenth), the first three in the line were born and educated in Central Tibet (Wu-Tsang).

The First, Gyalwa Gendun Drubpa, was born in 1391 in Tsang of a nomadic family. Semi-orphaned at the age of seven, his widowed mother placed him in Nartang Monastery near Shigatse, under the care of an uncle, Geshey Choshey by name, who was a learned Nartang monk. He studied there for a dozen years, and then went to the Lhasa area for further training. He made numerous meditation retreats throughout his life in both Wu and Tsang provinces, and after his enlightenment established Tashi Lhunpo Monastery in Shigatse, for training young disciples in the ten Buddhist branches of knowledge. Tashi Lhunpo is the main pilgrimage site today associated with the First Dalai Lama. He was both a prolific writer and builder; but his charisma as a teacher seems to have been his greatest asset, and during his lifetime he became the guru of almost everyone, from kings and queens to nomads and farmers, in Central and Southwest Tibet. His learning and enlightenment were so profound that he became popularly known as Jey Tamchey Khyenpa, or "The Omniscient Master." All future incarnations of the Dalai Lama lineage have this epithet, Jey Tamchey Khyenpa, prefixed to their ordination names.

Although the First Dalai Lama was profoundly learned, and after completing his studies spent many years practicing solitary meditation in retreat hermitages, his teachings always remained simple and practical. Perhaps this was the key to the great success he achieved.

In one of his poems of spiritual advice he wrote,

> When we continue to live without self-awareness
> And are driven blindly by past habits and conditionings,
> There is little space to experience deeper happiness
> Because of the negativity that we carry within.
> Seek instead for the nectars of inner peace and joy,
> The wisdom understanding ordinary and deeper levels of reality.
> Be humble and relaxed with the body and all things physical;
>
> With speech, drop all harsh and deceptive forms of expression;
> And with the mind, rest it in the spiritually beneficial,
> The primordial *dharmadhatu* awareness itself,
> Like a fish swimming in the boundless ocean
> Free from the hooks of attraction and repulsion.

His reincarnation, Gyalwa Gendun Gyatso, was born eleven months later, also in Tsang Province. His father was the head of the Shangpa Kargyu School of Tibetan Buddhism, and his mother a prominent leader of the Zhichey Tsarchod School. The latter spent forty-four years in meditation retreat during her lifetime, and was one of the great female mystics of her generation.

As a young boy the Second Dalai Lama was recognized as the First's reincarnation and was placed in Tashi Lhunpo Monastery for training. Tashi Lhunpo therefore is also an important pilgrimage site for events connected with the Second's life.

In his late teens our young monk went to Central Tibet for further studies, and entered Drepung Monastery near Lhasa. He made extensive retreats on Drak Yerpa Mountain to the northeast of Lhasa, as well as elsewhere throughout Central Tibet, and went on to become the greatest lama of his generation.

The Pagmo Drupa king, who ruled Tibet at the time, sponsored the building of the Ganden Podrang Monastic Complex within Drepung Monastery, which was to become the hereditary seat of all future Dalai Lama incarnations. Drepung, and in particular the Ganden Podrang within it, are therefore very important pilgrimage sites connected with the Second.

Later in his life he travelled to Southern Tibet, passing through the Yarlung Valley to Dakpo and Tsari. The return route from Tsari offers a detour up through the Olkha Mountains to the Lhamo Latso, the Lake of the female dharma protector known as Palden Lhamo. He took the opportunity to make this rigorous journey on all special occasions, on the way stopping to meditate in the caves at Olkha Cholung, where Tsongkhapa, founder of the Gelukpa School to which he belonged, had made a five year meditation retreat. On our pilgrimage we also camped below these caves and meditated in them.

On his second visit to the Lhamo Latso Lake he performed a sacred ritual, transforming the lake from a mere sacred pilgrimage place into a "Lake of Visions." From then until today, Central Asians make pilgrimage to and undertake a vision quest at this sacred lake.

He later built a monastery below the lake, known as Gyal. This became one of the great meditation monasteries from then until the Chinese Communist invasion of Tibet in the 1950s, and its subsequent destruction during the 1960s.

Our visit to this lake, and our vision quest there, was the highlight of the pilgrimage that produced the photos for this book.

In many ways the Second was the greatest of all the Dalai Lamas, and set the stage for what would be accomplished by future incarnations. The creation of his seat, the Ganden Podrang at Drepung Monastery, placed him at the heart of Central Asian spiritual life. He also established the link with the Nechung Oracle, and until today this oracle remains the main servant to the Dalai Lama institution. The founding of Gyal Monastery below the Lhamo Latso Oracle Lake was perhaps as important; from then until today the Dalai Lamas are popularly known as Gyalwa Rinpoche, the Gyal being derived from the name of that monastery. Moreover, from then until today, vision quests at the Oracle Lake have remained the principal means by which Dalai Lama incarnations are located and identified. The present Dalai Lama, for example, Gyalwa Tenzin Gyatso, was found by means of clues seen in this Lake of Visions by one of the lamas in charge of the search.

The Second was also a wonderful writer. He signed many of his poems with the epithet Long Nyon Gendun Gyatso, or "The Mad Beggar Monk Gendun Gyatso," to indicate that he saw himself as embodying the somewhat radical and counter-culture face of Tantric Buddhism. In one of his poems he wrote,

> Within the sphere of the finite and infinity,
> One fulfills enlightenment energy and wisdom.
> This produces the two dimensions of a Buddha,
> That spontaneously benefits both self and others
> In both conventional and ultimate ways.
>
> Merely thinking of these stages of enlightenment
> Fills the mind of this yogi with joy.
> Merely recollecting these profound spiritual experiences,
> Causes this yogi to swoon with delight.
>
> It moves me to give voice to this song,
> A melody of joyous experience;
> And to shuffle my feet to and fro
> In a dance of great inner ecstasy.

The Third incarnation, Gyalwa Sonam Gyatso, was in fact the first to be known by the name "Dalai Lama." He was born in the Tolung Valley to the north of Lhasa, and as a young child was ordained by Panchen Sonam Drakpa, who had been the main disciple of the Second Dalai Lama, and placed in the Ganden Podrang of Drepung Monastery for training. Like his two predecessors, he combined intense study with periodic meditation retreats, and eventually manifested his enlightenment.

The Third spent his early life in Central Tibet, first studying and meditating, and then teaching. He became head lama first of Drepung and then of Sera, and also made numerous retreats at Ganden, Drak Yerpa and Chimpu. In addition, he frequently visited Gyal Monastery to teach and make meditation retreat.

Our pilgrimage to the Oracle Lake took us through many of these sacred places.

Later in his life, in the mid 1570s, he was invited to travel and teach throughout the Mongol regions, and also the various kingdoms of Eastern Tibet, in Kham and Amdo provinces. In 1578 he arrived in Hohot, the southern capital of Mongolia (presently the capital of Inner Mongolia, i.e., one of the parts of traditional

Mongolia that have been under Chinese rule since 1921), where he met with Altan Khan and became the head of Mongolian Buddhism. He travelled and taught in the Mongol regions until his death in 1588.

In fact the Third Dalai Lama was the first to be known as "Dalai." Sometimes it is said that this is a title that was bestowed upon him by Altan Khan, but in reality no such title exists in Mongolian royal culture. The story is a simpler one.

At his childhood ordination into monastic life the Third was given the name Sonam Gyatso, or "Ocean of Creative Energy." Many years later, when he travelled and taught in Mongolia, the Mongolian king Altan Khan issued a proclamation declaring him to be the spiritual head of all Mongols. In this proclamation he translated the "Gyatso" part of the lama's name into Mongolian; Gyatso means "Ocean" or "Sea," and becomes "Dalai" in Mongolian.

The proclamation referred to him as Dalai Lama Dorjechang, or "Master who is an Ocean (of wisdom equal to) the Buddha Vajradhara Himself."

The Dalai Lamas have remained the head of Mongolian Buddhism from that time until the present day. Mongols today still refer to him as the "Dalai Baksha," or "Oceanic Master."

A half century later the Manchu Mongols conquered and colonized China. They too regarded the Dalai Lama as the head of their various schools of Buddhism, and continued the use of the name Dalai Baksha.

Westerners picked up the name "Dalai Lama" from them.

The Tibetans themselves did not use the name until recent decades. They prefer to use Gyalwa Rinpoche, "The Precious One from Gyal Monastery." Gyalwa is also a translation of the Sanskrit word *jina*, a synonym for "buddha." Thus Gyalwa Rinpoche can also be translated as "Precious Buddha." It works nicely for their favorite lama.

Some Tibetans also refer to the line of incarnations as Kundun, meaning something like "He Representing All Enlightenment Forces."

Like his predecessors, the Third was a prolific writer. When the time of his death drew near he called his disciples to meditate with him in the temple. He then gave them a last spiritual poem, with instructions for what they should do after his death.

One of the verses in this small text is especially touching. In it he wrote,

> Kyeh! For the benefit of others
> I have pretended to travel and teach.
> Although I moved daily from one place to another,
> I have never grown weary;

For during the long interval of my life
I have rested in the place of universal mind
And bathed in the radiance of reality itself,
Like the sun in a cloudless sky.
And reality is indeed the most wondrous radiance!
For in the mandala-like mirror of joyous mind,
The reflected objects of blissful awareness
Appear like a full moon in a clear autumn sky
Shining within a clear pool of water....
O friends on the way, take this, my final teaching.
Write it on a smooth white cloth
And hang it somewhere for all to see.
This would give me deep pleasure,
And perhaps inspire some of my friends
To turn their minds to the enlightenment path.

The group sat meditating all night in the temple. The Third Dalai Lama passed away the following morning, seated publicly in meditation, as the first rays of dawn appeared on the eastern horizon.

His reincarnation, the Fourth Dalai Lama, was born in Mongolia as a grandson of Altan Khan, and completed the work that had been initiated by the Third. He came to Tibet as a young man for training, and cemented the Tibet-Mongolia alliance that was now well under way.

His reincarnation, often simply called Ngapa Chenpo, or "The Great Fifth" by Tibetans, was the first in the line to become lama king. This occurred in 1642, and was a result of a century of continual conflict between the various kingdoms of the Tibetan Plateau. In addition to having the patronage of the various Central and Western Mongols (i.e., the Khalkas, Oriats and Dzungars), he also had the support of the increasingly powerful Manchu Mongols to the east.

Two years after the Dalai Lama became lama king of Tibet, the Manchu Mongols conquered China. In fact China remained a colony of the Manchu Mongols for the following three and a half centuries.

The Great Fifth visited Beijing in 1652 at the invitation of the Manchu Mongol emperor. The basis of the Tibet-Manchu-Mongolia alliance was established at that time, and remained in place until the fall of Manchu rule over China in 1911. At that time both Mongolia and Tibet issued declarations stating that none of the conditions of the treaty from this alliance would carry over to the new Han Chinese Republic.

The Great Fifth was perhaps the most mystical of all the Dalai Lamas. He constantly heard voices and received visions of great masters of the past, who would speak to him and give transmissions as clearly as scenes seen in normal waking life. His collected writings contain hundreds of titles, arranged in twenty-eight thick volumes. Twelve of the volumes deal with ordinary levels of Buddhist knowledge, and eight are dedicated to "inner" subjects. A further eight volumes are labeled as "secret," and generally were printed those editions of his works that were meant for general distribution. These eight secret volumes recount the transmissions that he received as *dak nang*, or "pure visionary experiences."

In addition to rising to the position of lama king over all of Tibet, the Great Fifth gave great energy to various building projects. These included the thirteen renovated monasteries, and the thirteen newly created temples. He also initiated the transformation of the fortress that King Songtsen Gampo had constructed on Red Mountain in Lhasa a millennium earlier into the Potala Palace, a most amazing building that towers over the city like a jewel at the center of a royal crown.

All Dalai Lamas, from the Fifth until the Chinese invasion of Tibet in the 1950s, made the Potala their primary residence. Of course as young monks in training they also spent considerable time in the Ganden Podrang of Drepung Monastery, but the apartment comprised of six small rooms on the roof of the Potala served as their primary home. The floor below this apartment contained numerous temples and chapels, and the floor below that housed the 120 monks of Namgyal Dratsang, the private monastic unit that had been established by the Third Dalai Lama in the Ganden Podrang.

A century later the Eighth Dalai Lama constructed a more modest facility as a summer residence. This was surrounded by a large park, and was really intended as a teaching site for the general public. Numerous scriptural transmissions and tantric initiations would be arranged here every summer, with either the Dalai Lama or one of his principal gurus leading the ceremony, and with thousands of people in attendance.

Although the Great Fifth lived a very busy life, he also dedicated considerable time to solitary meditation, and pressed his many disciples to do the same. In one of his many poems of spiritual advice he wrote,

> O you of good fortune who take to the spiritual path
> Through study, contemplation and meditation,
> Extend your vision beyond the insignificant things
> That benefit this one short lifetime alone.
> Stabilize your mind with sublime detachment
> And seek the enduring treasures of the spirit.
>
> Find yourself a hermitage large enough for just one person
> On a high mountain far from human habitation,
> A dwelling place fenced by meadows, forests and flowers,
> With your shadow as your only companion.
>
> The laughing sounds of running water
> And the gentle melodies made by wild deer:

These are the only sounds you need hear.
Then there is no chatter born from the three delusions
To act as a thorn to meditation.

After the Great Fifth passed away, his body was mummified and placed in a golden stupa inside the Potala. The bodies of all Dalai Lamas after him were similarly preserved by mummification, and kept inside stupas in the Potala.

When he died, however, his death was kept secret for twelve years. His official biography states that when he was on his deathbed he instructed his chief assistant, Desi Sangyey Gyatso, to maintain this secrecy in order to complete construction of the Potala. His reasoning was that the Tibetans would work enthusiastically if they knew he was behind the project, but would abandon the effort in his absence.

The ploy was successful , and the Potala was completed according to plan. It stands today as one of the greatest architectural achievements of Asia. In recent times it has been declared by UNESCO as a World Heritage Site.

Here it is perhaps sufficient to present brief portraits of these first seven Dalai Lama incarnations. We will see more on the subsequent incarnations in the pages to follow, when we visit the sites associated with their lives.

THE TIBETAN TRADITION OF KHORRA

Khorra literally translates as "circling" or "walkabout." It is the Tibetan term that is often rendered as "pilgrimage." A synonym is *neykhor* that translates as "circling power places."

I have led pilgrimage groups to Tibet once or twice a year for the past thirty years, as well as to sacred sites in Mongolia, Bhutan and China. In general I could say that khorra is my favorite Buddhist activity.

The 2003 pilgrimage to the "Sacred Sites of the Dalai Lamas," which culminated in our vision quest at Lhamo Latso, the Oracle Lake that is at the heart of the spiritual and secular power of the Dalai Lamas, ranks at the top of my list of all those spiritual adventures.

One of the participants, Michael Wiese, made a documentary film of this pilgrimage. It has been shown in art cinemas and at film festivals around the world, and stands as a wonderful record of the beauty and splendor that is Tibet, as well as of the magic that pervades the pilgrimage experience.

A SWORD CUTS THROUGH THE NET OF HESITATION,

AROUSES THE THREE WORLDS FROM THE SLUMBER OF DARKNESS,

AND ERADICATES THE POWERS OF IGNORANCE AND UNKNOWING.

SUCH IS THE IMPACT OF THE MELODIOUS SOUNDS OF ENLIGHTENMENT,

AWAKENING LIVING BEINGS FROM THE DEEP SLEEP OF DELUSION.

■ FROM *CRUSHING ALL NEGATIVE FORCES TO DUST*

THE FIRST DALAI LAMA, GYALWA GENDUN DRUPPA

1391-1475

CHAPTER ONE

THE KATHMANDU VALLEY

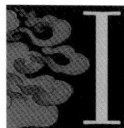

I LIKE TO BEGIN MY PILGRIMAGES TO TIBET FROM KATHMANDU. Most of the lineages of Buddhism that came to Tibet a millennium and a half ago, and that still survive today, came from India via the old trade route through Nepal. Many of these tantric Buddhist lineages are still preserved in their ancient Sanskrit forms with the Newar Buddhist masters of the Kathmandu Valley.

Legend states that the Kathmandu experience of Buddhism is far older than this, and goes back to the Buddha himself. The Buddha gave his transmissions in three essential forms: outer, inner and secret. The inner form refers to the *Prajna-paramita-sutras*, or "Discourses on the Wisdom Gone Beyond," that the Buddha gave to highly evolved masters known as nagas. These nagas then took them to "the bottom of a sea," where they quietly maintained them for five hundred years.

After that five hundred year period, when human civilization had become sufficiently ripe, the Indian master Nagarjuna travelled to this underwater sanctuary and retrieved the Wisdom Gone Beyond transmissions from the nagas.

The event was prophesied by the Buddha himself. In the *Descent to Langka Sutra* the Buddha says,

> Four hundred and fifty years after my passing
> An accomplished one (arjuna) whose name is Naga
> Will take birth in the south of Aryadesha (i.e., India).
> He will travel to the land of nagas, and will bring back
> My transmissions on the Wisdom Gone Beyond.

Contemporary Nepal Newaris believe that these nagas were ancient Newar mystics who lived in a cavern deep under the mountain on the west side of Kathmandu City, where the Swayambhu Temple presently stands. The legend is perhaps part of a far more widespread pan-Asian tradition of underground mystical cultures. Several of these are tied to legends of immortal sages. Kathmandu is linked to this esoteric legacy.

In prehistoric times the Kathmandu Valley was covered in a lake. A cave in the hills to the southwest of the city leads into a quagmire of underground caverns and tunnels. The Newaris believe that one of these hundreds of tunnels travels all the way underground to where the "naga masters" lived (and perhaps still live), and that it was to here that Nagarjuna travelled on his search.

The legend also links the Kathmandu Valley to Buddha's bodhisattva disciple Manjushri, to whom Buddha gave his deepest wisdom teachings. It is said that Manjushri visited the area long ago, and saw that it would eventually become the preserve of the Wisdom Gone Beyond teachings.

He took his sword and struck the ridge to the southwest of the city, opening a passage that allowed the lake to drain out.

Pilgrims today can visit the opening that Manjushri made at that time, and also can visit the entrance to the network of caverns that lead to the secret sanctuary under Swayambhu Mountain.

As mentioned above, the Kathmandu Valley has served as an important link on the trade route to Tibet since the earliest days.

While the Swayambhu Temple stands on the top of Swayambhu Mountain on the west side of the valley as a symbol of its primordial links to India and Indian Buddhism, an equally impressive temple stands to the east of the city. This is Baudanath, "Place of the Buddha." Over two thousand years ago, when much of Nepal was part of the Indian empire created by King Ashoka, Ashoka's own daughter spent several summers in Kathmandu to escape the Indian hot season. She built an elegant stupa to the east of the city, remnants of which still stand today. This was one of the 84,000 Buddhist stupas that Ashoka created across his newly established empire, that spread from Afghanistan on the north to Sri Lanka on the south.

Baudhanath Stupa was built half a mile to the east of this, as a meeting place for Tibetan and Newari traders.

These three great stupas – Swambhu, Baudhanath, and the stupa of Ashoka's daughter, are the three principal pilgrimage sites in the Kathmandu Valley today.

I like to begin every pilgrimage with a walk up the Swayambhu Hill. The 365 steps that lead up the hill to the temple complex on top are said to purify 365 lifetimes of negative karma. An alternative version states that each step purifies a day, so one walk up purifies a year of negative karma.

Either way, the climb is a great cure for jetlag. I usually take my groups there on the first day of their arrival in Asia, to get everyone centered and in tune with the spiritual adventure we are about to undertake.

In the travel literature of the 1960s and 1970s, in the early days of Nepal's opening to international travel, the temple complex at the top of the Swayambhu Hill became known as the Monkey Temple, because so many wild monkeys lived in the forest around it. However, the tribes of monkeys often harassed and even attacked visitors from abroad to steal fruit and other snacks that they would carry in open bags. Locals never had a problem with the monkeys; a good rock, well placed on the ass of the leader of the pack, would send the tribe scurrying; but Buddhist pilgrims from Japan and Korea, and of course Western tourists, were not familiar with this means of communication with our smaller primate cousins. After some hundreds if not thousands were scratched or even bitten in tussles over bananas and the like, the government decided that a simple intervention would be easier than educating the world of visitors on how to ward off monkey ambushes. They trap most of the monkeys and transplanted them in less frequented forests.

After the Chinese invaded Tibet in the 1950s, many tens of thousands of Tibetans fled into exile. The majority of them settled in India, but many thousands stayed in Nepal, mostly in the areas around these three stupas.

Almost from the time of their arrival they began to build Tibetan-style temples and monasteries. Fifty years ago there were only two or three Tibetan temples in the Kathmandu Valley. Today there are several hundred large and small ones. Nepalis from traditional Tibetan Buddhist regions such as Tamang, Mamang, Sharpa (of Everest) and so forth send their children to them for training. One can also find many young people from Sikkim, Bhutan and other Himalayan regions in them. And of course there are numerous Tibetan refugee lamas and youths.

A half dozen temples stand at the top of Swayambhu, some Tibetan and some Newari. Most pilgrims will spend a few hours here, turning the mantra wheels that encircle the great stupa at the center of complex, and passing through the small temples and chapels. They will then continue down the back end of the hill, that leads to several newly established Tibetan monasteries.

In recent decades the Tibetan refugees have also built numerous temples and monasteries on the taller hills behind Swayambhunath. In addition, they have worked with the local Newari Buddhists to build a long walk-around of the entire Swambhu Hill, with mantra wheels and small chapels along the way.

Anyone staying in the city for a longer period of time should make this circumambulation. Hundreds of Tibetans and Newaris make it every day, and on special occasions thousands and even tens of thousands do it.

IF ONE DOES NOT RETREAT TO THE MOUNTAINS

AND ACCOMPLISH THE PROFOUND AND INTENSE YOGAS,

TO REFER TO ONESELF AS A YOGI IS LIKE

A JACKAL IMITATING THE ROAR OF A LION.

■ FROM *CRUSHING ALL NEGATIVE FORCES TO DUST*

THE FIRST DALAI LAMA, GYALWA GENDUN DRUPPA

1391-1475

CHAPTER TWO

TSETANG AND THE YARLUNG VALLEY

T HE FLIGHT FROM KATHMANDU TO TIBET FLIES BY MOUNT EVEREST. Even on cloudy days, the peak of Everest pushes its way up through the clouds, and everyone on the plane presses toward the windows for a view.

Everest is the perfect metaphor for the contrast between Tibetan and Western culture. For the West it is the most famous mountain in the world for climbers and adventurers. Westerners who visit here generally do so in order to connect by osmosis with the fame and glory of those who have ascended to its peak.

The Tibetan name for Everest is Chomo Lungma. This in fact is the name of a mountain deity. Central Asians make pilgrimage to Chomo Lungma in order to visit the sacred sites on the base of the mountain, such as the cave where the Indo-Pakistani master Padma Sambhava meditated in the mid eighth century. Another popular site is the spring where Padma Sambhava's tantric sex partner and principal disciple Yeshe Tsogyal meditated and bathed.

This contrast in spiritual attitude between Westerners and Tibetans was markedly visible at many of the places we were to visit on our pilgrimage.

The plane lands in Gongkar Airport, near Lhading. The name "Lhading" literally means "Playground of the Gods." Most visitors to Tibet take the hour drive from here either across the mountains and then downstream along the Kyichu River to Lhasa; or else they choose to go upstream along the Yarlung Tsangpo River to the Yarlung Valley.

I prefer to begin my pilgrimages in Yarlung, for both historical and aesthetic reasons. Historically the culture that we think of today as the Tibetan civilization comes through and was inspired to new heights by the line of kings who ruled from Yarlung. Secondly, from the aesthetic point of view, Yarlung is still recognizably Tibetan, and has not been buried by the onslaught of Chinese immigrants to the extent that Lhasa has.

The young Second Dalai Lama passed through Yarlung on a teaching tour in the mid 1490s, when he was in his early twenties. This was his first visit since his predecessor studied, practiced, and then taught here many decades earlier, and it was an emotional experience for him. He describes his initial impression in a poem,

Magnificient Yarlung, a picture of wonder
Sketched by the brush of celestial artisans,

With forests rustling in ever-cooling breezes,
Lines gently flowing like those on a hand;
Beautiful towns, villages and temples
Set like pearls in delightful display;
Its fields like outstretched wings of a parakeet in flight
Laden with gems of ripening crops:
Kyehu! It is as though the kingdom of paradise
Has found its way to this northern land of ours.

Of course the Chinese Communist destructions of the 1960s and 1970s have brought about considerable transformation for the worse, but one still gets brief glimpses of the beauty that the Second Dalai Lama is describing.

Another verse by the Second in the same epic poem mentions the two main pilgrimage sites in the valley,

Here on the face of the sacred Mount Potala
Stands the splendid Yarlung Castle,
Its walls emanating great bursts of light
Like a palace built by divine craftsmen
From stones formed from the dust of precious jewels;
And, in front of it, the Dradruk Temple,
An edifice magically manifest from the wisdom
Of Lokeshvara, the Buddha of Compassion.

According to Tibetan legend, the Yarlung Castle was originally built in the second century B.C. by the man now known as the First Yarlung King, Nyatri Tsenpo. The name means "Lord Carried on a Planquin." According to the legend, a small group of foreigners appeared one day in Yarlung. Most accounts suggest that they were a small Indian army, fleeing a civil war that they were losing in their homeland. The Tibetans asked them where they were from. The leader of the group, not knowing the Tibetan language, made the traditional Indian gesture indicating non-understanding; he pointed his index finger at the sky and twisted his wrist.

The Tibetans, not understanding that this simply meant non-understanding, took it to mean that he and his followers had descended from the heavens. They put him on a palanquin and carried him to their village, where they declared him to be their king. (Some readers will note that Rudyard Kipling was inspired by this tale to create a British Raj novel, *The Man Who Would Be King*; the book was later made into a movie, with Sean Connery and Michael Caine playing the starring roles.)

Legend states that this first king was an emanation of Avalokiteshvara, the Buddha of Compassion. He built the Yarlung Castle, and brought the various nations of the Central Asian Plateau under his rule. Because he was an emanation of Avalokiteshvara, the mountain became known as Truzin, a Tibetan translation of

Potala; this is the name of the mountain in South India traditionally associated with Avalokiteshvara. Any place where Avalokiteshvara or any of his emanations live becomes known as a "Potala." The Potala Palace in Lhasa has its name from this same reasoning.

Later Tibetan literature would identify King Nyatri Tsenpo as a former incarnation of the soul destined to become the Dalai Lama. This mythology was not widespread in the time of the Second Dalai Lama, for the Dalai Lama institution was still very much in its formative stages. Hence he would probably not have been aware of it when he wrote his poem.

The second sacred site mentioned in the Second Dalai Lama's poem is the Dradruk Temple. This was created many centuries later by the thirty-third king of the Yarlung Empire, Songtsen Gampo by name. I mentioned him briefly in the introduction.

Songtsen Gampo expanded the Tibetan empire tenfold, pushing its borders deep into Nepal and India on the south, through much of Kashmir on the west, deep into China on the east, and including much of the Silk Road of the Western Gobi to the north.

After creating this vast empire he sent a group of twenty-five scholars to India to devise a new script that would be used throughout his many lands, replacing the hodgepodge of scripts used in the diverse areas at the time. The resultant product was the Tibetan script that has come down to us today, pretty much in the form in which it was devised fourteen hundred years ago. That script is still used through most of these regions, including Bhutan, Ladakh, Mongolia and so forth.

Songtsen Gampo also declared Buddhism to be the national religion, and he built 108 temples throughout his land. According to the legend, he believed that all of the lands he had conquered and united under his rule were in fact territories of a great Earth Goddess. He had these 108 temples built at sacred places on her body, so that she would consent to serve as a protectress of his empire.

The Draduk Temple in Tsetang of the Yarlung Valley was amongst the first dozen of these 108. It was also one of the most elegant and lavish, for the thirty-two generations of his royal ancestors had all lived and ruled from here. In addition, he had the Yambu Lagang Palace at Yarlung transformed into a temple, and it remains as such today.

Songtsen Gampo was the last of the Yarlung kings to rule from Yarlung. After creating a vast empire he moved his capital northwest to Lhasa, which had better access to the regions to the far north, west and east.

The Yarlung Valley and environments have dozens of pilgrimage sites that Tibetans love to visit, for the legends go back in time far beyond human history.

Just outside of the city stands a second Potala Mountain. Myth states that hundreds of thousands of years ago a monkey was meditating in a cave high on this mountain. An abominable snowlady fell in love with him, and eventually the couple united. They produced six children. These were the first humans to appear in our world, and all other humans are descended from them.

This somewhat Darwinian take on the origin of humans contrasts sharply with the traditional Indian Buddhist belief that humans are descended from *akinista* beings, i.e., beings from another world, namely the celestial realm of Akinista.

Again, like King Nyatri Tsenpo and Songtsen Gampo, this monkey too was an emanation of Avalokiteshvara, the Buddha of Compassion, and thus was an early incarnation of the soul destined to become the Dalai Lama.

A wonderful Buddhist female monastery stands at the foot of this hill, built on the side of a cave in which King Songtsen Gampo meditated for several years as a young man.

Tibetans make circumambulation of this sacred mountain *en masse* on special days of the month and year. Some locals do it on a daily basis, usually at either dawn or sunset.

The temple and stupas built on this Darwinian mountain as commemoratives of the monkey and abominable snowlady were destroyed by the Chinese Communists in the 1960s and have not been rebuilt. The dozens of temples referred to in the poem by the Second Dalai Lama were also destroyed at that time, with most still not rebuilt. The Yarlung Castle was also destroyed, but has been somewhat rebuilt.

The Draduk Temple is one of the thirteen of Tibet's 6,500 temples and monasteries that were not totally destroyed by the Chinese Communists at that time. Instead it was converted to military purposes during the Communist Purges, and only given back to the Tibetans in the early 1980s, after the death of Chairman Mao.

 LL EXISTING THINGS ARE INTERDEPENDENT,

AND ALL THINGS THUS LACK ANY SEPARATE BEING.

CULTIVATE THIS VISION; AND BE AWARE OF THE WORLD

AS ILLUSORY, LIKE A MAGICIAN'S CREATIONS.

■ FROM *MEDITATIONS TO PREPARE THE MIND FOR TRANSITION*

THE SECOND DALAI LAMA, GYALWA GENDUN GYATSO

1475-1542

CHAPTER THREE

THE LHASA EXPERIENCE

LHASA HAS PERHAPS SUFFERED MOST DEEPLY from the Chinese Communist invasion, and one needs to maintain a sharp focus in order to retain a sense of it as being in Tibet. The Tibetan population of Lhasa in 1949, the year I was born, was somewhere around 100,000, with perhaps a hundred Chinese traders and diplomats. Today over a million Chinese immigrants have flooded the city, and the Tibetans are very much out-populated in their own capital. The drive into Lhasa from the airport goes through mile after mile of new Chinese construction. And the flood of Chinese immigrants continues to build utilitarian Communist architecture that is ubiquitous, all created over the past four decades. Chinese army posts can be seen at most intersections around the old parts of the city, each manned by a half a dozen soldiers in full battle fatigue, and complete with a machine gun nest fortified by sandbags.

That said, the discerning pilgrim can still establish a pilgrimage link to some of the great power places that served as the main source of Tibet's spirituality and culture for the past fourteen hundred years, and that are so profoundly linked with the lives and enlightenment deeds of the Dalai Lamas for the past six centuries.

The most important, of course, is the Potala Palace, which is built on Red Hill at the very center of the Lhasa Valley. King Songtsen Gampo created the basis of this building when he moved the capital of Tibet from the Yarlung Valley to Lhasa. The Lhasa Valley was more centrally located for the administration of his newly established empire.

He probably chose the Red Hill for his new palace because of a small cave found on it. Although he was a military man on the scale of Julius Caesar before or Chinggis Khaan after him, he was a profoundly spiritual person, and spent months every year meditating in the sacred caves of Central Tibet as part of his vision quests for inspiration on how to forge and later how to administer his empire.

One of these caves was located on Red Hill in the center of the Lhasa Valley, and his visions there inspired him to build his new residence around it. This is the so-called "White Palace."

A thousand years later, when the Fifth Dalai Lama was made lama king of the country, he added the section that is now known as the "Red Palace."

During my years of Buddhist studies in India I supported myself and my family by writing articles for newspapers and magazines. A frustration with these medias is that they tend to add whatever story titles they like, as well as whatever story descriptions. I remember that one year, when I submitted an article to *Macleans Magazine* in Canada from an interview I did with the Dalai Lama, they added a descriptive blurb stating something like "Until 1959 the Dalai Lama lived in the Potala, a fabulous 1,000 room palace in Lhasa." The suggestion was that he lived a lifestyle somewhat like the kings of France in the Versailles.

The reality was very different. In fact the Dalai Lamas owned an apartment comprised of six small rooms on the roof of the Potala, two of which were meeting rooms – one larger one for holding audiences with groups; and a smaller one, which served as a waiting room for people coming to see him privately. The four in which he lived are approximately twelve feet by twelve feet in size, indeed modest in size. The total area of these six rooms is smaller than that of a house owned by a simple middle class European or North American family.

The other "1,000 rooms" were dedicated to other purposes. For example, the floor below contains numerous temples and chapels, mostly containing stupas housing the mummies of the Fifth to Thirteenth Dalai Lamas. Below these are the residences of the 120 monks of Namgyal Dratsang, the small monastery created by the Third Dalai Lama, that the Fifth brought with him when he moved from the Ganden Podrang of Drepung Monastery into the Potala. And below these are the rooms of the Tibetan government administration, as well as what in effect was the National Archives.

My favorite chamber in the Potala is the chapel dedicated to the Seventh Dalai Lama, probably because he is my favorite of all in the line of incarnations. His mummy sits inside an elegant stupa here, and three statues of him look on from the side: one depicting him as a young boy, one depicting in mid life, and the third depicting him how he looked the year before he passed away.

Fortunately the Potala is one of the thirteen traditional buildings that was spared destruction by the Communists during the 1960s, and its dozens of chapels remain more or less intact. Of course it is run by the Chinese as a museum, rather than as the temple complex and monastery that is its traditional function; but pilgrims look beyond this formality, and use it as a pilgrimage site.

Strangely, although the Potala is a celebration of the life and enlightenment deeds of the various Dalai Lama incarnations, photos of the present Dalai Lama are forbidden in it, as elsewhere in Central Tibet. At least, this is the case at the time of writing.

Until the Chinese invasion of the 1950s, the Potala dominated the Lhasa skyline, and could be seen from miles away. Today the Chinese have built hundreds of high rise buildings for the tens of thousands of Han immigrants that they are sending in, as well as dozens of enormous hotels, this latter as part of their plan to turn Tibet into a kind of scenic Disneyland for the burgeoning Han middle class.

This Chinafication of Tibet contrasts starkly with the Tibet that was crafted by King Songtsen Gampo in the mid 600s, and that endured for thirteen centuries. In particular, two of the policies devised by Songtsen Gampo profoundly affected the direction that Tibetan culture was to take, and in very clear terms set it apart from Chinese culture.

The first of these was the decision to establish and patronize Indian Buddhism as the national religion of Tibet. Modern social anthropologists suggest that he did this in order to create a homogenous spiritual and cultural foundation for the hundreds of petty kingdoms and nomadic tribes that he had recently united. This meant building many dozens of Buddhist temples and monuments, importing Buddhist teachers from various neighboring countries, and sponsoring the translation of hundreds of Buddhist scriptures.

His second pivotal decision was to create a new script to be used throughout his empire, and to have this script based on Indian Sanskrit rather than on either Persian or Chinese, the scripts used by his large neighbors to the west and east respectively.

In essence, these two policies meant that from his time until the twentieth century, a period of more than thirteen hundred years, Tibet evolved as an Indian cultural satellite.

A century or so later one of his descendents, King Trisong Deutsen, took the policy a step further, and banned official use of the Chinese script in Tibet, as well as the translation of books from Chinese. This policy effectively locked China out of Tibet as a significant culture influence for centuries to come. Of course when the Khalka Mongol Kublai Khaan conquered and colonized China in the 13th century, and later the Manchu Mongols colonized China in 1644, the Tibetan lamas gained intimate glimpses into Chinese secular culture; Tibet's alliances with these two Mongol super-powers, both of whom followed Tibetan Buddhism, and both of whom colonized China, were such that the Tibetan lamas served as official tutors to the Khalka Mongol and Manchu Mongol royal families.

It is interesting to note that King Songtsen Gampo and King Trisong Deutsen, who pressed these two important policies, are both considered to be prior incarnations of the Dalai Lama. This is stated in a prayer written by Reting Rinpoche in 1939. After the Thirteenth Dalai passed away in 1933 Reting was appointed as his regent; he oversaw the search for the young reincarnation, and then the enthronement of the boy in 1939. Reting wrote a long-life prayer to be chanted at the enthronement ceremony (the full text of which we have included as an appendix to this book.)

The prayer opens with the following verses,

> In order to fulfill the wishes of the buddhas and bodhisattvas,
> You accepted to incarnate here in Tibet,
> The northern land ringed with snow mountains,
> And first came as a line of kings who illuminated
> The land's affairs on both temporal and spiritual dimensions.
> To list but a few of these Dharma kings incarnations,
> There was King Nyatri Tsenpo, King Tori Nyanshal,
> And the great emperors who made Buddhism the national religion:
> Songtsen Gampo, Trisong Deutsen and Tri Ralpachen.

Thus both Songtsen Gampo and Trisong Deutsen are clearly mentioned in this passage as being prior incarnations of the Dalai Lama.

Two other sites in Lhasa's old city are of special note: the Jokhang Temple, and the Ramochey Temple. Both were built by Songtsen Gampo in the mid 600s, more or less at the same time that he created the Palace on Red Hill. In particular, he built the Jokhang for the Nepalese princess whom he had taken as one of his five wives; and he built the Ramoche for the Chinese princess whom he took some years later as another of his five wives. His other three wives were Tibetan; the Crown Prince, and the son who became his royal successor, was born from his first Tibetan wife.

Every Dalai Lama, from the First until today, has spent time in both of these temples, either as a young monk attending teachings, as an older monk giving teachings, or simply to lead prayer ceremonies or make pilgrimage.

Somewhat ironically, during the Cultural Revolution of the 1960s the Chinese Communists confused which temple had been built for which princess. As mentioned earlier, during this period they destroyed all but thirteen of Tibet's 6,500 monasteries and temples. The thirteen they did not destroy were temples having some connection with Chinese history. The only exception of which I am aware is the Tara Temple built by the Bengali master Atisha in roughly 1050; when the Thirteenth Dalai Lama was in India between 1909 to 1913, he gave responsibility for this temple to the King of Bengal. This seems to have saved it from destruction; the Bengali government during the Chinese Cultural Revolution was a democratically elected Communist Party, and Mao did not want to offend it.

As mentioned above, in the Chinese Communist mania to destroy all visages of traditional culture, they confused the history of these two great temples; and in their blunder they destroyed the Ramoche, the temple that had been built for the Chinese princess, and saved the Jokhang, the one built for the Nepali princess.

The Jokhang is the singularly most sacred destination for all Central Asians on pilgrimage in Tibet. In fact, most Central Asians regard it as second in importance in the world only to Bodh Gaya, Buddha's place of enlightenment in India.

Although the Jokhang was closed by the Communists from the early 1960s until after the death of Chairman Mao, it reopened in the early 1980s. As for the Ramoche, it was completely destroyed; but it has been somewhat rebuilt and once more serves as an important pilgrimage destination.

The Lhasa Valley has dozens of other pilgrimage sites. One of these is Ani Sangku, the female monastery built around an underground cave where Songtsen Gampo liked to meditate in the hot season after moving to Lhasa. Later when Lama Tsongkhapa, founder of the Yellow School to which the Dalai Lamas belong, visited and taught in Central Tibet, six of his female disciples established a small but elegant meditation hermitage. It was destroyed by the Communists, in the 1960s, but has been rebuilt.

Another important pilgrimage site connected with King Songtsen Gampo lies on the mountain ridge north of Lhasa. This is the great Pabongkha, with a cave where first Songtsen Gampo and a century later Guru Padma Sambhava meditated. Every Dalai Lama has spent time here. According to legend, Songtsen Gampo built two towers here, one for each of his two foreign wives. He had a rope bridge built connecting the roofs of the two, and during his meditation retreats at Pabongkha would make nightly excursions between the two to make love with them. The monastery here was destroyed by the Communists, as were the towers. The monastery has been partially built since the death of Mao.

A sky burial site lies a few hundred meters below Pabongkha, where Lhasa people bring their dead to be cut up and offered to the vultures as a final act of generosity on the part of the deceased.

The three hour walk along the northern ridge from Pabongkha to Chusang Gompa, another female monastery, climbs up the mountain to Tashi Choling Hermitage. Here the great Pabongkha Dechen Nyingpo attained enlightenment and became the greatest teacher in the Yellow School of Tibetan Buddhism during the first half of the twentieth century. Another hour hike will bring one down to Sera Monastery, directly north of Old Lhasa.

Sera was one of the two great Yellow School monasteries in the Lhasa Valley, the other being Drepung. All Dalai Lamas have spent time in these two monasteries, and the Third was abbot of one and then the other before he left to teach in the Mongol regions in 1578.

Another great walk in the Lhasa Valley is from Drepung to Nechung.

Drepung was the largest monastery in Old Tibet, with over 10,000 monks in its various departments. Moreover, as mentioned in the Introduction, the Second Dalai Lama made the Ganden Podrang in Drepung his primary residence, and also identified it as the *labrang* or "incarnate seat" for future Dalai Lamas. The statues of the various Dalai Lama incarnations in the main assembly hall at Drepung are spectacular. This monastery was once several miles to the northwest of Lhasa; but the new Chinese settlements have now extended Lhasa all the way to Drepung and beyond.

It takes a couple of hours to pass through the many chapels and temples of Drepung, with the Great Assembly Hall being the *grand finale*. One can then stroll along and down the hillside to Nechung Monastery, following the old pilgrimage route.

Prior to the Communist invasion of Tibet, Nechung was the home monastery of the State Oracle, known in Tibetan as the Nechung Kuten, or "Human Vessel Channeling the Nechung Deity." All Dalai Lamas from the time of the Second have relied heavily upon advice given in trance by the Nechung Oracle, and the Oracle is consulted in the search for every Dalai Lama incarnation. The Great Fifth Dalai Lama made the Nechung Oracle the official State Oracle of Tibet; and from the time of the Seventh Dalai Lama the monk serving as the vessel channeling the Oracle (i.e., the man who channels the deity Pehar Gyalpo, also known as Dorje Drakden) has been given a government title.

The walk from Drepung to Nechung follows the old pilgrimage route, and offers clear views of the new Chinese constructions in Lhasa.

Many pilgrims to Lhasa today make day trips to the great monasteries, temples, hermitages and meditation caves of the outlying areas around Lhasa. In olden times each of these outings could take several days, but with modern roads and Land Cruisers can now be easily completed in a day. Most of these monasteries and temples were destroyed by the Communists during Mao's rule, but many have been rebuilt since his death.

Some of the most important of these are Drikung Til, the head monastery of the Drikung Kargyu School; Tsurpu, the seat of the Karmapa Lamas and thus head monastery of the Karma Kargyu School; Ganden Monastery, that was founded by Tsongkhapa and thus was the first monastery of the Gelukpa School; Reting, the monastery established by Lama Drom Tonpa, and that served as the head monastery of the Kadampa School; and Drak Yerpa, the cave and temple complex where Central Tibetans of all schools have meditated for many centuries.

These days one can also make day trips from Lhasa to Samye, Mindroling and Dorje Drak, three of the six most important monasteries of the Nyingma School. Again, these were destroyed in whole or in part during the Cultural Revolution, but have been rebuilt to some extent and are again active monasteries.

As said earlier, a pilgrimage to Lhasa is at one and the same time profoundly inspiring and also overwhelmingly heartbreaking. The sacred sites of the Dalai Lamas are still there, but even the Dalai Lama's photograph is banned in them; and they have become so crowded by Han Chinese immigrants and the Communist urban sprawl that one has to keep one's mind in meditative concentration not to be distracted by the tragedy.

THIS HUMAN LIFE WITH ITS FREEDOMS AND ENDOWMENTS

IS A SUPREME VESSEL FOR SPIRITUAL TRAINING.

THINK OVER THE PRECIOUS OPPORTUNITY THAT IS YOURS

AND TAKE ADVANTAGE OF IT, O SEEKER OF TRUTH.

■ FROM *SONG OF THE ENLIGHTENMENT PATH*

THE SECOND DALAI LAMA, GYALWA GENDUN GYATSO

1475-1542

CHAPTER FOUR

THE KANGYUR STUPA AND THREE LHASA CIRCUITS

LHASA HAS THREE CIRCUMAMBULATORY ROUTES AROUND THE JOKHANG, the heart of the old city. These are known as the Inner Circuit (*Nang Khor*), the Intermediate Circuit (*Barkhor*), and the Outer Circuit (*Chi Khor*, also known as the *Ling Khor*).

The Circuit is inside the Jokhang Temple complex. One has to enter the main doorway of the temple to undertake it, and this is not always open to the public. When one walks through this entranceway, one finds oneself in a large courtyard. Prior to the Chinese invasion of Tibet, the Dalai Lama (or in his minority his regent) would often lead prayer ceremonies in this courtyard. The Jokhang Temple stands at the other end of the courtyard. The whole complex is surrounded by a high wall, with a few meters between the wall and the temple. This forms a natural route for pilgrims to follow in circumambulating the temple. Hundreds of *mani khorlo*, or "mantra wheels" line the circuit, and Tibetans love to turn these and recite mantras as they walk. Both the temple walls and the outer walls are covered in hundreds of fresco paintings on this inner khorra. Some of those paintings illustrate historical events connected with the temple, whereas others are celebrations of the buddhas and bodhisattvas.

Most pilgrims to the Jokhang make a walkaround of this inner khorra three times before entering the temple.

Thousands of Tibetans stand in line for a walkthrough of the Jokhang on religious occasions. The long line snakes its way through the dozens of chapels that make up the temple. Most pilgrims carry pots or bags with vegetable oil, adding a few spoonfuls to the butterlamps as they go. As a result, the floors are rather slippery, for not all the oil makes it into the lamps.

The Jokhang gets its name from the main statue in it, known as the Jowo. But this is only one of hundreds of statues in the dozens of chapels in the Jokhang. Tibetan pilgrims will sometimes offer a coat of gold leaf to the faces of the most sacred of the images as part of their pilgrimage, as an act of good karma. This gold is one of the main supports of the temple. Every few days the layers of gold on the statues become so thick that it has to be scraped off to make room for more.

The popularity of the Jokhang, and its power as a symbol of the Tibetan spiritual, cultural and historical identity, has placed it at the forefront of the rebuilding efforts that have characterized life in Tibet since the death of Chairman Mao.

In general it could be said that the Inner Circuit is a purely spiritual experience. The halls and chapels are small, and one is carried through them by the flow of the crowd. There is little opportunity for chatter, socializing or distraction.

Tibetans are enthusiastic pilgrims, and on special days the pushing and squeezing can be a tad unsettling for a novice to the experience. For example, when the Dalai Lama gave personal blessings after a Kalachakra initiation in India in the early 1970s, several people were crushed to death in the push to be at the front of the line. The same thing happened a few years later in Ladakh, when three people died from the crunch. Something of this enthusiasm can be felt in the air on special days in the Jokhang, with every person in the crowd pushing fiercely to get to his or her most cherished chapel before all the blessings have evaporated.

The Intermediate Circuit, or Barkor, begins directly in front of the Jokhang, and follows a circular route around it. The complex that is the Jokhang is protected by high outer walls, probably in the old days to keep out thieves or wandering armies. Most Tibetan monasteries and temples doubled as forts in times of war. The Barkhor follows along the outside of this, and takes a half hour or so to walk. Tibetans regularly walk it with great enthusiasm several times every morning and evening.

Much of the spiritual action happens in the square in front of the temple, which has two large incense cairns. Pilgrims toss an offering of any of a number of aromatic substances on the fire as they pass. Juniper branches are popular, because of their wonderful smell. Roasted barley flour is another favorite, as is barley wine. Tibetans call the tradition *sang chok*, meaning "rite of smoke." The ritual comes from ancient times, when shamans performed smoke offerings as a means of paying respect to and maintaining harmony with local mountain spirits. The Central Asian Buddhists adopted these practices from their ancestors. North American shamans have a similar rite that they brought over with them when they migrated from Central Asia thirteen thousand years ago.

Whereas the inner circuit is exclusively spiritual, the Barkhor doubles as an outdoor market. Several hundred shops open in the mid morning, and stay open for business until sunset. This does not disturb the pilgrims, for they do most of their circumambulating during sunrise and sunset, before and after the shops open and close. A hundred years ago international visitors to Lhasa commented on the wide array of things that could be found in this market. The same is true today, although the casual visitor will mainly see bric-a-brac from China, India and Nepal, by Chinese businessmen immigrants to sell to countryside Tibetans who are visiting the city. Tourists and international pilgrims, of course, are also among the buyers.

The Outer Circuit, known as the Ling Khor, encircles the old part of Lhasa, from the Jokhang on one end to the Potala on the other. Thousands of Tibetans walk this on religious occasions, many stopping in front of the Potala to offer prostrations to the visualized Dalai Lama.

The route also passes around Chakpori, the hill on which the Fifth Dalai Lama built a national medical college, known as the Menzukhang. This was destroyed by Mao during the 1960s, and now has a television transmitter where the medical college once stood. However, the base of Chakpori Mountain has numerous sites of interest to pilgrims.

One is a cave where Songtsen Gampo meditated in the early 600s. It has also been used for meditation by many great lamas over the centuries, including many of the Dalai Lamas. A small hermitage stands below it, that in better days was used by monks of the Dalai Lama's monastery for meditation retreats. This was also destroyed by the Communists, but has been rebuilt in part.

One very interesting structure is known as the Kangyur Choten, or "Stupa of Buddha's Words in Translation." The Kangyur is a collection in 108 volumes, of the roughly one thousand discourses of the Buddha that were translated into Tibetan. Here local rock cutters have worked for the past decade and a half, carving the words of these 108 volumes into slate "pages." The flat pieces of slate are then piled and arranged in the shape of an enormous stupa. Just below it, other artists have painted images of numerous buddhas and bodhisattvas on the face of a boulder as large as a four or five story house. All of the work at this site is the brainchild of a wonderful bearded Drukpa Kargyu lama from Kham, East Tibet. Pilgrims passing by the site make offerings toward the effort. It has been most wonderful to witness the progress year by year, and of course also a great honor and source of merit to have been able to make small contributions to the work on each of my visits.

Most Tibetans complete the Ling Khor in three or four hours. Tibetan pilgrims from the remote countryside often make the circuit while doing *kyang-chak*, or full length body prostrations. For this one takes a pebble in ones hand, prostrates the length of one's body, leaves the pebble to mark the place, takes two steps toward the pebble, picks it up, and prostrates again. Needless to say, these pilgrims take considerably longer to complete the full circuit.

The Ling Khor, or "The Ling Circuit," gets its name from four monasteries that mark the outer periphery of the route in the four directions. Each of these monasteries has the syllable "Ling" in its name. These were used as residences of the teachers of the child Dalai Lamas. A teacher would often become more commonly known by the name of which of the four monasteries he lived in than by his personal or ordination name.

Many Tibetans make the Ling Khor circumambulation every day for the first two weeks of Saka Dawa, the Buddhist holy month. This usually begins with the new moon of May; but the date on the Western calendar can vary, because the Tibetans follow a lunar calendar, and their Leap Year leaps a month. Then each succeeding year for the next three years is a week shorter than the Western year.

**I** SEND FORTH THE PURE ASPIRATION

THAT I MAY TRANSCEND THE NEGATIVE HABIT

OF DISCRIMINATING BETWEEN LIVING BEINGS,

REGARDING SOME WITH AFFECTION AND OTHERS WITH AVERSION;

AND THAT INSTEAD I MAY LEARN TO HOLD THEM ALL

WITHIN THE MEDITATION OF LOVE AND COMPASSION

THAT CHERISHES OTHERS MORE THAN EVEN ONESELF.

■ FROM *SONG OF PURE ASPIRATIONS*

THE SECOND DALAI LAMA, GYALWA GENDUN GYATSO

1475-1542

CHAPTER FIVE

SAMYE AND BEYOND

TIBETAN BUDDHISM IS PRESERVED IN SCHOOLS OR SECTS OF TRANSMISSION. In general it is said that there are four great schools — Nyingma, Sakya, Kargyu and Gelukpa (this latter also known as "The Yellow School" because of the yellow hats that its monks wear during special ceremonies) — but in reality there are several dozen sects. The Kargyu School alone, for example, has twelve subdivisions.

The reason for this great diversity is the vast distances between individual Tibetan valleys, and the difficulty of travel in the pre-modern world. Each monastery and valley developed something of its own uniqueness in the manner in which the enlightenment legacy is communicated, in the balance between philosophical study and meditative endeavor, and even in terms of linguistic expression.

Sometimes the schools are divided into two main movements: those that developed prior to the eleventh century, and those that emerged in the great renaissance of the eleventh and twelfth centuries. The former are known as Nyingma, or "Old Schools," and the latter as Sarma, or "New Schools." The Sakya, Kargyu, Kadam and Geluk are in the latter category.

Three of the great Nyingma Monasteries lie between Lhasa and Yarlung: Samye, Mindroling and Dorje Drak.

Samye, which was built in the mid 700s, is generally called "Tibet's first monastery." In reality there were several hundred temples and monasteries before this time; for example, King Songtsen Gampo alone built 108 of them, and the building fury was continued by his successors.

However, these are not classified as "Tibetan monasteries," for two main reasons.

The first is definition. A temple (Tib., *lha kang*) can be built anywhere; but a monastery (Tib., *gompa*) should be at least three earshots in distance from any city, town or village. Moreover, a monastery must have five or more fully ordained monks in order to qualify for the name "monastery," and not be a mere temple or hermitage. This is because it takes five fully ordained monks to perform the ceremony for ordaining new monks.

A second reason is that the earlier temples in Tibet were not maintained by Tibetan Buddhist monks or nuns, but by monks and nuns hired from Tibet's many Buddhist neighbors: India on the south, Kashmir on the West, Khotan on the North, and China on the east.

Then in the mid 700s King Trisong Deutsen decided to create Tibet's first monastery. He brought the Indian master Shantiraksha and a quorum of monks able to conduct the ordination ceremony. Seven young men were chosen for the task. As a result, they became Tibet's first seven monks, and Samye became Tibet's first fully qualified monastery. (Of course in all probability numerous Tibetans had become monks or nuns prior to this time; but it seems that there were never enough to create the required minimum of five to make up a qualified quorum.)

Another important event at this same time was the importation from India of Shantiraksha's nephew, the great tantric master Padma Sambhava. Although not a monk, Padma Sambhava assisted Shantiraksha in the work of creating Samye Monastery. Every Nyingma Monastery and Temple in Tibet today has statues of these three beings: Padma Sambhava, Shantirakshita and King Trisong Deutsen. As mentioned earlier, King Trisong Deutsen is regarded as an prior incarnation of the Dalai Lamas. Thus he is also a reincarnation of Songtsen Gampo, his ancestor who made Buddhism the national religion of Tibet and created 108 temples across the country.

In future centuries Padma Sambhava would come to greatly eclipse Shantirakshita in popularity in the Tibetan mind, and today is regarded as the founder of the Nyingma School. Of course this is largely symbolic. Buddhism had been in Tibet for many centuries before him, and had even become the national religion a century earlier. But he is the solitary figure who stands out above all others as the embodiment of the sentiment and the approach to enlightenment that is seen today as characterizing the Nyingma School.

In another sense he is also the forefather of all Tibetan schools, in that all later schools arose from the fertile ground created by the Nyingma movement.

The Nyingma School today is less monastic than the various Sarma Schools, and has many great lamas who are married or have girlfriends. That said, its monasteries are as strict in the practice of Vinaya celibacy as the monasteries of other schools.

Samye served as the primary seat of the Nyingma School for many centuries. Later it was considered too important to be associated exclusively with any one school, so became more of a trans-sectual facility. This movement began in the thirteenth century, when the lama Chogyala Pakpa became the guru of the Mongolian emperor Kublai Khaan, and the latter gave Tibet as a present to the former. Chogyal Pakpa and the succeeding Sakya lamas ruled over Tibet as lama kings, but in general did so without any sectarian bias. However, they saw Samye as bigger and more important than any one school, and so pushed it in an independent direction. Later, when the Fifth Dalai Lama became lama king of Tibet in 1642, he continued this policy.

Samye Monastery is probably the most important pilgrimage destination in Central Tibet after the Jokhang and Ramoche Temples of Lhasa.

The pilgrimage to Samye from Lhasa requires a boat ride. One follows the road from Lhasa to the airport, and then turns left along the northern bank of the Yarlung Tsangpo River toward Tsetang. This is the same road that we will take later when we travel to the Oracle Lake.

A half hour before arriving at Yarlung one stops at a ferry crossing, and takes a boat across the river. The boat ride is maybe a half hour in length when the river is high, but is much longer in dry season, when the river is shallow and the boatmen must avoid silt buildups. The ride offers wonderful views of the valley and surrounding mountains.

Samye was designed after a Buddhist mandala, with four gates leading into it, and the temple as a celestial palace at the center. Because it was sponsored by the Tibetan king and built largely by Tibetan craftsmen, yet used architects from both India and China, its three stories pay honor to these three Buddhist civilizations: one floor is in Indian style, another in the Tibetan, and the third in the Chinese.

Perhaps even more dramatic than Samye is the retreat hermitage of Chimpuk, built a couple of miles behind it. This is the mountain on which Padma Sambhava placed dozens of his Tibetan disciples in a twelve year retreat. Twenty-five of them attained realization, and became known to history as "the twenty-five *siddhas* of Chimpuk," siddha being the Sanskrit title for an accomplished tantric master. Most Nyingma temples have a set of paintings of Padma Sambhava with these twenty-five masters. Sometimes, as in Samye Monastery, the twenty-five appear as wall frescoes.

Mt. Chimpuk hosts a cave complex on its higher reaches. Padma Sambhava placed his closest disciples in a twelve year retreat in these. Today these caves are primary pilgrimage destinations. The walk up to them is not easy, for the foot of the mountain lies at an altitude of some 12,500 feet, and it is a steep climb up from there.

A favorite cave of every pilgrim is that of Princess Yeshe Tsogyal. According to legend, as a young woman Yeshe Tsogyal was so exquisitely beautiful that several barons were about to go to war for her hand in marriage. To avert the conflict, King Trisong Deutsen intervened and made her his fifth wife, for none of the barons would dare challenge his might.

Later, when Padma Sambhava arrived, Yeshe Tsogyal requested to be given to him as travel companion and assistant. The two immediately became lovers. The caves in which they practiced meditation and the sexual yogas are very popular with all Tibetans, even (and perhaps especially) with the monks and nuns, who share vicariously in the mythology.

Readers familiar with Tibetan art will know that paintings of Padma Sambhava often depict him with two women standing or seated beside him. One is the Indian princess Mandarava, and the other the Tibetan princess Yeshe Tsogyal. Both were his lovers.

He is said to have met Mandarava when teaching in Zahor, a small kingdom at the foot of what today is the Manali-Kullu Valley in Himalayan India. The king of Zahor had invited him to come and teach in his court. The king's daughter, Mandarava, was a nun at the time, but that did not deter Padma Sambhava. One day

Padma and Mandarava went missing. The search party discovered them in a cave on the mountain above the town, caught in the act of making love.

The king was furious, and ordered them to be burned alive for their behavior. A pyre was built in the center of the town, and they were tied on top of it. The fire was ignited, and a great cloud of smoke came forth. Eventually the smoke became so thick that the town had to be evacuated.

When the smoke cleared and people returned, they discovered that the town was now covered in a lake, with a lotus island at the center. There sat Padma Sambhava and Mandarava, naked and unharmed.

Padma Sambhava's sexual enthusiasm continued in Tibet, where he is said to have made love with hundreds and perhaps even thousands of female disciples. The chief of them, however, and his principal Dharma heir, was Yeshe Tsogyal. The caves in which they meditated and practiced the sexual yogas are legendary.

After Padma Sambhava departed from Tibet Yeshe Tsogyal became his successor, and oversaw the organization of his lineages and teachings into the legacy that has come down to us today.

Padma Sambhava's private cave on Chimpuk is also highly revered, as is that of Vairotsana. Vairotsana was one of the twenty-five siddhas, and was the main translator of the period. He oversaw all the translation projects that Padma Sambhava initiated, and also wrote extensively on Padma Sambhava's oral instructions to him and others.

Mongol pilgrims to Chimpuk pay special attention to the caves of Tamdin and Lhapel, two of the twenty-five siddhas. Mongols call these two masters by the names Sokpo Tamdin and Sokpo Lhapel (Sokpo meaning "Mongolian"), and claim that they were both Mongols who returned to Mongolia after their training under Padma Sambhava was complete.

A wonderful female monastery stands at the foot of Chimpuk. It was destroyed by the Communists in the 1960s, but is has been partially rebuilt and is very active today.

Two other great Nyingma monasteries lie within a few hours travel of Samye and Yarlung. Perhaps the most important is Mindroling, for it has produced many of the greatest lama scholars in the Nyingma School over the past few centuries. The frescoes in this monastery of the lamas in the *dzogchen* lineage are especially wonderful. *Dzogchen* is a unique transmission of the wisdom trainings in the Bon and Nyingma Schools of Tibetan Buddhism. These two schools term it as the highest of all the teachings that they maintain.

The other great Nyingma monastery in the region is Dorje Drak. It too was destroyed by the Communists, but has been somewhat rebuilt and is once more an active monastery.

In olden times each of these pilgrimage sites would take a day or more to visit, but modern roads and means of transport place them today within a few hours of each other.

THE BODY AND MIND, CLOSE COMPANIONS FOR SO LONG,

ARE PULLED APART WHEN THE LORD OF DEATH STRIKES

AND ARE FORCED TO GO THEIR SEPARATE WAYS.

WHAT TO SAY THEN OF WEALTH, RELATIVES AND FRIENDS?

YOU DESTINED FOR WHITE HAIR, LIKE A HEAD COVERED IN SNOW

AND FOR A FACE CARVED WITH WAVES OF WRINKLES,

YOU SHOULD ACCOMPLISH THE WISDOM OF ENLIGHTENMENT RIGHT NOW,

AND THEN THE ETERNAL YOUTH OF A JOYFUL SOUL WILL BE YOURS.

■ FROM *A NECKLACE OF JEWELS*

THE SECOND DALAI LAMA, GYALWA GENDUN GYATSO

1475-1542

CHAPTER SIX

DRAK YERPA, THE HEART OF SACRED MOUNTAINS

IAM SOMETHING OF A CAVEMAN, and my three favorite pilgrimage sites in Central Tibetan are mountains with great cave complexes that have been used by mystics for centuries, perhaps even millenniums. The three are Chimpuk, Drak Yerpa and Terdrom. We saw Chimpuk in the previous chapter, and will see Terdrom later.

Drak Yerpa, located approximately a one hour drive northeast of Lhasa on the road to Reting, perhaps tells the Tibet story more fully than any other mountain in Tibet. Its meditation caves were used in ancient times by the Bonpos, and later by almost all the great Buddhist masters in Central Tibet's mystical history.

As we saw earlier, King Songtsen Gampo married two foreign Buddhist wives in the mid seventh century, and created 108 Buddhist temples around the country. He is said to have meditated in the caves on both Chimpuk and Drak Yerpa, and to have built another dozen Buddhist chapels and monuments on these two sacred mountains. His cave on Drak Yerpa is especially revered.

The recorded history of these two sites begins at this time with Songtsen Gampo, for earlier written records of the area were destroyed in the wars of the seventh and eighth centuries. However, the fact that he meditated in the caves at both places is a strong indication that their history goes back far beyond that time, and that they had been used by the Bonpo shamans and Bon Buddhists far earlier.

Drak Yerpa is really a mountain range at the top of the Yerpa Valley, rather than a single mountain. That said, all of the important pilgrimage caves are on the mountain at the front of the range, with views overlooking the Yerpa Valley.

The mountain itself is said to be an embodiment of the female buddha Tara, known in Tibetan as Dolma. One does need some imagination to see the likeness. Lamas point out how one part of the mountain resembles Tara's left leg, which is tucked into the meditation posture, and another resembles the right leg, stretched out in the heroine posture; in this way, Tara symbolizes how we should always rest the mind in calm meditation, while at the same time being fully active for the benefit of the world. King Songtsen Gampo embodied this dual role; as a king and conqueror he was very active in shaping the world, but at the same time he cultivated inner peace by means of meditation.

Other parts of the mountain symbolize Tara's shoulders, neck, head and so forth. Finally, at the place on the mountain where her vagina would be on her body, a spring of sacred nectars flows forth. Tibetans drink this spring water, convinced of its healing properties.

The pilgrimage route on the mountain climbs up and to the left. There, where Tara's right shoulder would be, the first cave one comes to is associated with Yeshe Tsogyal, Padma Sambhava's lover and Dharma heir; she is said to have come here on pilgrimage with her parents when she was a child. She left her tiny footprint in solid rock, to indicate that even at the tender age of nine she carried the blessings of the buddhas and bodhisattvas.

Above this is the cave where the Bengali master Atisha, founder of the Kadampa School of Tibetan Buddhism, lived and meditated in the mid eleventh century, with five hundred disciples scattered in caves along the mountain range behind. The cave of his chief disciple Lama Drom Tonpa, another previous incarnation of the Dalai Lamas, immediately adjoins that of Atisha. The Kadampa School inspired the renaissance that gave rise to all later schools of Tibetan Buddhism, and elements of it can be found in every school and sect of Tibetan Buddhism today. Much of the early Kadampa literature emerged from the masters living in these caves at that time and over the generations to follow.

Two caves on the mountain are associated with Padma Sambhava. One of these is very near the mountain peak, and is not on the official pilgrimage route. The other is much lower, and situated where Tara's left shoulder would be. This is the cave he used to teach King Trisong Deutsan, Yeshe Tsogyal and the dozens of other disciples who made the retreat with him here. It is often called "The Flying Cave," because Padma is said to have flown from and back to his cave for each of the teaching sessions.

At the place on the mountain where Tara's right breast would be is the cave of the Three Wrathful Bodhisattvas, and at the site of the other breast is the cave of the Maitreya Cave of the Fifth Dalai Lama. Tara's full breasts represent how the enlightened beings always enrich the world with the milk of enlightenment energy; the Three Bodhisattvas and also Maitreya perform this action on behalf of all buddhas past, present and future of the ten directions.

My favorite cave on the mountain is known as Kalzang Drakpuk, which gets its name from the Seventh Dalai Lama, Gyalwa Kalzang Gyatso. The Great Seventh, my favorite of all the Dalai Lamas, made retreat and attained realization here. The cave is far above the standard pilgrimage route, and is clothed in prayer flags, so considerable effort must be exerted to visit it. The last time I visited it, two monks from Kham were making the three year retreat in the cave. The Kalzang Drakpuk is in fact two caves: one that the Seventh Dalai Lama used for meditation; and the other, where his attendant stayed to take care of him.

The smaller mountain to the right of Drak Yerpa is known as Lhari Nyingpo, "The Heart of Sacred Mountains." Pilgrims generally picnic here after finishing the circuit of Drak Yerpa. Atisha often taught on Lhari Nyingpo during his retreat on Drak Yerpa, and after his death his disciple and Dharma heir Lama Drom continued the tradition. A simple stone seat here is known as "Drom's Throne." Lama Drom used it during his years here to give public discourses to large groups of disciples. Traditionally the Dalai Lamas, as reincarnations of Lama Drom, sit on it and teach during their visits to Drak Yerpa.

The walk around the top of Lhari Nyingpo passes by a sky burial site, where local Tibetans bring their dead to be cut up and offered to the vultures. Drak Yerpa is somewhat remote, so the local vultures are not offered as many feasts as are the vultures living near Pabongkha, where we saw another sky burial site in an earlier chapter.

Actually, "sky burial" is a Western name for the ritual of feeding a dead body to the vultures. The Tibetans call it *ja tor*, or "bird offering." Most people would choose this as the most auspicious means of leaving the world. Of course divinations and astrological charts would be done on behalf of the deceased, and sometimes these would suggest cremation, burial in the earth, or burial in water (i.e., a lake). In general, however, the bird offering was the preferred method. Birds are emanations of the dakinis, or angellettes, and having them take one's body and carry it (albeit morsel by morsel) into the sky and in the direction of the heavens, was and is considered to be an auspicious ending to the life story of most human beings. Far better than feeding it to worms and insects under the earth, or to fish in the sea; and more environmentally friendly than cremation, which requires a considerable amount of wood.

THE EXPERIENCE OF THE TANTRIC YOGI IS LIKE THIS:

THE OUTER WORLD IS SEEN AS A SACRED MANDALA CIRCLE,

AND ALL LIVING BEINGS SEEN AS DIVINE BEINGS.

ALL EXPERIENCES BECOME TRANSFORMED

INTO THE BLISSFUL PRIMORDIAL AWARENESS;

AND ALL OF ONE'S ACTIONS BECOME SPIRITUAL,

REGARDLESS OF HOW THEY CONVENTIONALLY APPEAR.

EVERY SOUND THAT ONE MAKES

BECOMES PART OF A GREAT COSMIC SONG.

■ FROM *SONG OF TANTRIC EXPERIENCE*

THE SECOND DALAI LAMA, GYALWA GENDUN GYATSO

1475-1542

CHAPTER SEVEN

THE SAKYA PATRIARCHS

IN THE CHAPTER ON DRAK YERPA we encountered the caves of Atisha, Lama Drom Tonpa (another pre-Dalai Lama incarnation), and the early Kadampa masters, who adopted the caves of the Drak Yerpa range as their main place of meditation and teaching. After Atisha passed away Drom and his disciples lived here for some time, but later many of them moved to Reting. Here they first meditated in the caves of the area, but later built an amazingly beautiful monastery.

The Kadam School that emerged from their work became a major spiritual and philosophical force during the renaissance of the eleventh century. This movement is especially interesting because Atisha, in addition to his Indian training, had travelled to Indonesia and studied there for twelve years. He widely propagated these Indonesian lineages in Tibet, and they are still preserved today. These lineages are of great interest to historians, for the Muslim invasions of Indonesia a few centuries later destroyed the enlightenment tradition in that country, and these transmissions have survived only in the Tibetan transmissions.

Although numerous schools emerged during this renaissance, perhaps the most important both spiritually and culturally after the Kadampa was the Sakya. The name literally translates as "Gray Earth," because of the color of the clay in the area. It is said that when Atisha came to Tibet in 1042 he followed the old trade route from Nepal that passes below the Sakya Valley. He turned in the direction of the valley and offered three prostrations. He then made a prophecy that a great spiritual tradition would emerge from there.

At that time the soul destined to become the Dalai Lamas was embodied in the form of Lama Drom Tonpa, who became Atisha's principal Dharma heir. It was Drom who organized Atisha's lineages and doctrines into what became the highly successful Kadampa School of Tibetan Buddhism.

After Drom passed away he was reborn in the Sakya area as Kunga Nyingpo, the son of Khon Konchok Gyalpo. Khon Konchok Gyalpo, a married Buddhist teacher, had studied with many masters, including the great Drokmi Lotsawa. In 1073 he established a monastery at Sakya in order to house the various lineages he had received. Of special importance were the tantric lineages that his guru Drokmi Lotsawa had gathered, such as those of the Indian mahasiddhas Avadhutipa and Virupa.

Over the generations to follow, Sakya Monastery rose to become a major force in the spiritual renaissance that was sweeping Tibet. Lama Drom's reincarnation as Sakya Kunga Nyingpo was a major reason for this success. Just as Drom had taken the lineages of Atisha and organized them into the highly successfully study and practice program that became the foundations of the Kadampa School, his reincarnation as Kunga Nyingpo now did this with the diverse lineages that his father had planted in Sakya Monastery.

Kunga Nyingpo made eighteen years of meditation retreat and gained enlightenment. During one of his retreats he received a vision, in which all the enlightenment teachings were presented as four simple lines.

> If attached to worldly vicissitudes, you have no commitment to truth;
> If attached to conditioned experience, then no personal independence;
> If attached to self-purpose, no perspective of the universal hero;
> And if you accept (things as they appear), then no ability to really see.

Later he wrote eleven commentarial texts to these four lines, one for each of his eleven principal disciples. Known as "Separation from the Four Bondages," these four instructions are codes for meditation methods often practiced for weeks, months or even years by Sakya adherents today.

Kunga Nyingpo was not the only Sakya pre-incarnation of the being who was destined to be reborn as the Dalai Lama. Several generations later,

Kunga Nyingpo's great grandson Chogyal Pakpa took birth and rose to become head of the Sakya School. He too was a Dalai Lama pre-incarnate.

Chogyal Pakpa was the first Tibetan lama to come to the attention of the West. Marco Polo met him when he visited Mongolia in the late 1200s, and he plays a prominent role in Marco's *Journals*. (Yes, Marco Polo never visited China; he visited Khaanbelik, or modern-day Beijing, which Kublai Khaan set up as the capital for the administration of the eastern part of the Mongol Empire that he had forged. This empire included Korea, the Manchu Mongol territories, much of Mongolia, northern Vietnam, eastern Russia, and so forth. China was just one of Kublai Khaan's many colonies.)

Sakya literature speaks of "The Five Early Sakya Forefathers." These are sometimes referred to as "the three whites and two reds," because three were married and therefore wore white robes, while two were celibate monks and therefore wore the traditional red robes for which Tibetan lamas are most famous.

Of the two Dalai Lama pre-incarnations, Sakya Kunga Nyingpo was one of the "whites," and Chogyal Pakpa one of the "reds." Atisha's main disciple Lama Drom Tonpa had also been a "white." Thus numerous of the pre-Dalai Lama incarnations were lay yogis, and not celibate monks.

Sakya is famous for many things with pilgrims. One of these is its "wealth vases." The monastery manufactures various kinds of vases, which are filled with auspicious substances and then consecrated by the monks by means of many hours of mantra and prayer. At the time of our visit, three different types were available: *nor bum*, or "abundance vase"; *lu bum*, or "harmony with nature spirits vase"; and *namchu bumpa*, or "essence of all good things vase. Pilgrims will often buy one or more of these and take them to their homeland, either keeping them in a high place in the house, or sometimes (and with some types of consecrated vases) burying them in special places on the property.

As mentioned in the Introduction, the special relationship between Central Mongols, Manchu Mongols and Tibetans was created in the early days of the Sakya School, with the Mongols as patrons and protectors of Tibet, and in return the Tibetans supplying lamas to the Mongol courts as teachers of Buddhism, and as "priests" to perform the various kinds of Buddhist rituals used throughout the far east, such as healing and abundance rituals, death and transmigration rites, and so forth.

Kublai Khaan also instructed Chogyal Pakpa to create a simplified Tibetan script for use throughout his empire. Known as *Pakyig*, it was used for a few decades. In fact, Kublai planned to ban the Chinese pictorial script altogether from use in China and Korea, and replace it with the phonetic *Pakyig*. Unfortunately this policy was not successful.

Eventually the *Pakyig* script fell into disuse even with the Mongols. Mongolia had been largely Tibetan Buddhist for many generations, and preferred the more classical Tibetan script to which everyone was accustomed. In addition, Mongol lamas often went to Tibet for higher education, and had to use the classical script during those periods. The *Pakyig* soon fell by the wayside, and today is just an historical footnote.

MOST PEOPLE PASS THEIR LIFE GATHERING

EPHEMERAL POSSESSIONS THAT SOON WILL BE LOST.

THEY EXERT GREAT EFFORTS AND ENDURE GREAT HARDSHIPS FOR THEM.

YET THESE THINGS ARE LIKE TRACES LEFT BY A BIRD IN FLIGHT,

OR LIKE DRAWINGS MADE ON FLOWING WATER.

PERHAPS IT IS UNDERSTANDABLE FOR AN IGNORANT FOOL

TO DEDICATE HIS OR HER LIFE TO SUCH SUPERFICIAL PURSUITS;

BUT HOW TRAGIC WHEN THOSE WHO KNOW OF ENLIGHTENMENT DO SO

AND THROW ALL DEEPER SPIRITUAL GOALS TO THE WIND.

■ FROM *SONG OF THE WISDOM TRANSMISSION*

THE FIFTH DALAI LAMA, GYALWA LOZANG GYATSO

1617-1682

CHAPTER EIGHT

A MILAREPA CAVE

AS MENTIONED IN AN EARLIER CHAPTER, I especially love pilgrimage to the meditation caves of Tibet that are associated with great mystics of the past. The *Mahayana Sutra Alamkara* describes eight qualities that every meditation hermitage should have; Tibetan meditation caves usually have these to the highest degree. We have already visited many of these caves in Yarlung, Lhasa, Chimpuk and Drak Yerpa.

The renaissance movement of the eleventh century produced many schools, such as the Kadam and Sakya, that we saw in previous chapters. Another is the Kargyu School. Our pilgrimage route would take us to the Milarepa cave and temple complex near Nyelam, on the road from Lhasa through Tsang to Nepal. Milarepa is one of the early Kargyu forefathers, and is popular with all schools of Tibetan Buddhism. He was a great poet and song writer, often expressing his enlightenment teachings in verse. The Kargyu has its roots in the work Milarepa's guru, known as Marpa Lotsawa, or "Marpa the Translator."

Marpa was a rather eccentric mystic from Lodak in South Tibet, which is a few days walk from the Milarepa cave near Nyelam that we would visit. He first began his Buddhist studies with the Tibetan masters of West Tibet, but then went to India and continued his training under several great tantric masters there. The most important of them was Naropa. Stories of Marpa's austere training under Naropa are popular with all Tibetan lamas.

Back in Tibet Marpa transmitted his lineages to numerous disciples. Milarepa was the most famous of these.

After spending many years at the feet of Marpa Lotsawa, Milarepa embarked on a series of long retreats in the caves of the Himalayas, from the Mon areas of the eastern Himalayas, to Mt. Kailash on the far west. His many mystical songs and poems are collected into a volume famed as the *Mila Gurbum*, or *One Hundred Thousand Songs of Mila*.

Neither Marpa nor Milarepa were monks. To the contrary, Marpa is said to have kept a wife and eight mistresses. Milarepa lived a more simple sexual life and never married nor kept long-termed mistresses, but he did practice the sexual yogas with "the five healing sisters" while living in retreat to the north of Mt. Everest. There is some debate over whether these were human girls or celestial maidens; after five years of solitary meditation in remote caves, one can see how even an unwashed provincial farmer girl could be mistaken for a gift from the gods.

Milarepa in turn had many disciples, but the most important of them was the monk Gampopa. It was Gampopa who formulated the teachings of Marpa and Milarepa into the structure that has come down over the generations as the various Kargyu Schools. Gampopa was a monk in the Kadampa School, and united these lineages with those that he received from Milarepa. As a result, the Kargyu School is sometimes referred to as a "Union of Two Streams," meaning the lineages from Marpa's Indian masters, with those from Atisha and the Kadam School.

The Kargyu produced the largest number of sub-sects of any Tibetan movement. Gampopa had four chief disciples, each of whom established a monastery in his homeland. These eventually evolved into its own sub-sect, the four collectively being known as "The Four Older Kargyu Lineages." His most important disciple was Pakmo Drupa, who similarly had eight chief disciples, each of whom established monasteries and hermitages. Again, each of these developed into its own sect, and the eight collectively became known as "The Eight Younger Kargyu Schools." Sometimes this is translated as "Four Greater" and "Four Lesser," but the meaning is simply older and younger. The four older are about 900 years old, and the four younger about 875, so there is not alot of difference in their ages. In fact the largest and historically most important is the Drikung Kargyu, one of the eight younger, that at times was as large as all other Kargyu sub-sects combined.

Each of these twelve Kargyu sub-sects had its own head lama or "Throne Holder," and operated completely independently of the others. This probably came about because of the huge distances between them, and the difficulty of travel over high mountains. But as the centuries passed, each of them developed something of its individual linguistic, as well as subtle variations in philosophical and meditative training systems. Today each maintains its own body of literature, manages its own training programs and retreat facility, has its own master scholars and retreat masters, and so forth.

All of the Dalai Lamas received numerous lineages that have come down from Milarepa. The Seventh Dalai Lama, himself a wonderful poet and song writer, expressed his enthusiasm for these lineages in a song,

> High on the snowy peaks of the Himalayas,
> A yogi pursued intense meditation
> And burned the forests of the inner distortions.
> Through skilful method, his wisdom soared
> In the sky of truth, the way things are.
>
> His name was Milarepa, the people's delight,
> And Shepei Dorje, "The Laughing Vajra."
> He was a mountain towering over all other yogis.
> At his golden feet I offer this song
> To cause the vital energy of realization
> To enter the drop of vajra life at the heart….
>
> In the skies before me, the wisdom of bliss and void
> Manifest as a field laden with precious jewels

And adorned with every kind of medicinal plant,
With beautiful lotuses and kingly trees filled
With serene birds that delight the mind.

There on an antelope skin sits Milarepa,
The Laughing Vajra, at the mouth of a mountain cave.
He is radiant with lights of five colors,
Legs crossed in the meditation posture,
And body with a greenish blue hue.
A vajra song flows forth from his lips,
Melodiously resounding far and wide.

Wondrous yogi who attained the vajra body,
Whose voice attained the sixty qualities of a buddha,
And whose mind attained the glorious enlightenment
Of great bliss spontaneously fully aware of all things,
O marvelous yogi, I offer this song to you.

The cave near Nyelam is one of the first where Milarepa meditated after leaving Marpa's hermitage. According to the story, after many years of training with Marpa, the latter one day gave him a final instruction, and then told him to go and find places of solitary meditation. For the next eighteen years Milarepa did this, and blessed numerous caves across the southern Himalayas with his presence.

He came upon the Nyelam cave by chance. He was passing through the area, and the local people asked him to perform some weather control rituals for them. Their crops had been badly damaged by storms for several years running, and the community was in a difficult situation. He moved into the cave to perform the rituals, and took a liking to it. The weather in the valley immediately changed for the better, and the local community was deeply impressed. They requested him to stay, and promised their support. He remained meditating in this cave for a couple of years.

At one point while living there, the area was struck by a small earthquake. An enormous boulder, several tons in weight, became dislodged from the ceiling of the cave. Milarepa jumped below the boulder and held it up, while his disciple Rechungpa put a supporting rock under it. The places where Milarepa's hands and shoulders touched the boulder sank into the rock like a knife into butter. Visitors to the cave love to touch these, and compare the size of their hands with those of Milarepa.

Milarepa's great disciple Rechungpa Lotsawa was with him at the time. His cave is smaller than Milarepa's, but almost equally sacred. Like Marpa, Rechungpa travelled to India many times and brought back his own lineages from various teachers there. On one of these journeys Milarepa instructed him to find and bring back the healing yogas of the *Amitayus Tantra*. Rechungpa did this, and later transmitted them to Milarepa.

These lineages became almost as famous and widespread in Tibet as the Milarepa lineage known as the Six Yogas of Naropa. The First Dalai Lama wrote an extensive lineage to the former transmission, while the Second Dalai Lama wrote a treatise on the Six Yogas.

Our pilgrimage group included a Bhutanese monk. Some years earlier he had created a kind of monk rock opera on the life of Milarepa, and staged it for locals in Bhutan. He had brought copies of one of the Milarepa songs with him, printed in phonetics, and requested the twenty-one members of our pilgrimage group to sing it with him.

I am not sure that Milarepa would have been pleased by the melody we created that day, a disparate group of North American and European pilgrims trying to follow a Bhutanese interpretation of a Tibetan mystical song. But I think he would have been impressed by the effort.

Meypa! Self-discipline is the earth in which to plant the seed;

The power of meditation provides the moisture and nutrient;

And the training in wisdom is the sunshine to ripen the crop.

In this way one's spirit matures, producing

An inner harvest that utterly eradicates

Every semblance of spiritual sickness and poverty.

■ from *Song of the Wisdom Transmission*

The Fifth Dalai Lama, Gyalwa Lozang Gyatso

1617–1682

CHAPTER NINE

OLKHA CHOLUNG AND A JUNIPER BERRY ENLIGHTENMENT

THE MODERN ROAD FROM LHASA TO LHAMO LATSO, the Oracle Lake, runs to the Gongkar Airport, then by Mindroling Monastery and Yarlung. This is very different than the old route that the Second Dalai Lama took when he first visited Lhamo Latso in the early 1490s. His pilgrimage took him through Samye, and then back over the high mountain passes. But horses and yaks can go where Land Cruisers fear to tread.

A few hours beyond Tsetang the road passes near the Olkha Cholung Valley. This valley is famous with pilgrims for the meditation hermitage where Lama Tsongkhapa, founder of the Gelukpa, meditated for five years with eight of his early disciples in the late 1300s. Lama Tsongkhapa was also the main guru of the young First Dalai Lama, although the two were to meet many years after Tsongkhapa's meditation retreat in Olkha, and so many subsequent Dalai Lamas came here to make retreat.

All schools of Tibetan Buddhism that emerged prior to Tsongkhapa had their roots directly in particular Indian masters: the Nyingma School in Padma Sambhava; the Kadam in Atisha; the Sakya in Virupa and Avadhutipa; and the Kargyu in Naropa and Tilopa.

Tsongkhapa, on the other hand, did not look directly to India for his training and inspiration, but instead studied in forty-five different Tibetan monasteries, and with fifty-five of the greatest Tibetan masters of his time. In establishing the Geluk Tradition, he brought together the best lineages that he found in all of them.

Thus the Geluk School that emerged from his work was Tibet's first truly eclectic school.

It also became known as the Yellow Hat School. Whereas monk scholars in the older schools wore a pointed red hat when leading religious rituals, Lama Tsongkhapa adopted the yellow hat that had been in use in the Sakya sub-sect associated with Shalu Monastery in Tsang. Three hundred years later the Mongols abbreviated the name "Yellow Hat School" to "Yellow School," when they made the Geluk their main tradition in the late 1600s.

Tsongkhapa had in fact been born far from Central Tibet. His homeland was the Kokonor region of Amdo, a couple of thousand kilometers northeast, on the border of Tibet and Mongolia. His father was a Mongolian aristocrat with a title from the time of Kublai Khaan, and his mother a Tibetan. At the age of four he received the traditional hair-cutting ceremony from the Fourth Karmapa, the head of the Karma Kargyu sub-sect, and then become a monk under the tutelage of a Sakya monk, Rendawa by name. He came to Central Tibet for higher studies when he was in his late teens, and remained there for the rest of his life. As part of his training in Central Tibet he studied in all the greatest monasteries of the day, including Drikung (the head monastery of the Drikung Kargyu), Sakya (head of the Sakya), Reting (head of the Kadampa), Shalu (head of the Shalu School).

After a decade of studies he passed through Olkha Cholung on pilgrimage with eight of his disciples, and took up residence in the caves there. The local king was impressed by their presence, and built a small practice hermitage for them just below the caves. That hermitage was destroyed by the Chinese Communists in the 1960s, but has since been rebuilt.

According to oral tradition, Tsongkhapa and seven of the eight disciples undertook the practice of *chulen* during the five year period of the retreat, eating only a handful of juniper berries a day. Chulen is a tantric tradition, in which the practitioner takes a small amount of food or liquid, and by means of mantra and visualization turns it into vast feast. The term *chulen* literally translates as "the extraction (*len*) of quintessential nutrient (*chu*)."

Several forms of *chulen* existed in Tibet. The First Dalai Lama wrote a small text on living on essence extracted from purified mercury, and another on extracting nutrient by breathing in starlight at night. He himself did retreats in which he practiced these two methods.

Another famous method uses flower essence pills. The Second Dalai practiced this, and wrote a text on it. One makes small pills out of roasted barley flower, dried flower petals, and some auspicious substances. One then consecrates these by means of mantra and meditation. During the retreat one eats only a handful of these each day, and abstains from all coarse food altogether. While living in Dharamsala in the 1970s I knew two Tibetan yogis who lived exclusively on these flower essence pills for several years. One of them even became somewhat chubby from the practice, although he probably only ate the equivalent of a few tablespoons of the essence pills a day, and abstained altogether from all ordinary food.

A fifth method is called *doyi chulen*, or "extracting the essence of stone." One places a pebble in a glass of water, recites mantras to call universal essence into it, releases the essence into the water, and then drinks the water. Again, one abstains from coarse food throughout the extent of the retreat.

After Tsongkhapa and his eight disciples took up meditation in Olkha Cholung, the local king noticed their presence and came to pay his respects. He offered to build a small hermitage for them just below the caves, where the group could meet for communal practice on special days. This endured until the Chinese Communist destructions of the 1960s and 1970s, when it was destroyed. However, replicas were rebuilt after the liberalization of the 1980s, and today a small monastery adorns the site.

We had the good fortune on our visit to discover that a lama from the Jokhang in Lhasa whom I had known for many years had been sent to Cholung as resident teacher to the young monks. He graciously led us through the cave complex, and sat with us in meditation in Tsongkhapa's sacred cave.

On one of his many visits to Olkha Cholung the Second Dalai Lama composed a poem,

> To train under a lama accomplished in the Great Way,
> To penetrate to the meaning of the sutras and tantras,
> To extract the essence of this precious human life by cultivating
> Personal enlightenment, that benefits both self and others:
> This is what it means to meet with the wondrous lineage
> Of Lama Tsongkhapa, a lord amongst masters.
> This is not so bad, really, as a way to go.

The caves at Olkha Cholung, where Tsongkhapa and his eight chief disciples made this extraordinary five year retreat, do not have the towering heights of the meditation caves at Drak Yerpa or Chimpuk, that we visited earlier. However, they have the great blessings of being the first hermitage where Tsongkhapa made his first long retreat. Later he would make extensive retreats in the Lhasa, including at Rato, Drak Yerpa and Reting; and then would build the great Ganden Monastery on Nomad Mountain, to house his lineages. The hermitage at Olkha Cholung, however, would always remain special among equals.

The traditional pilgrimage route to the Oracle Lake cut through the high mountains directly behind Tsongkhapa's retreat cave in Olkha Cholung. After Tsongkhapa's retreat here, the Olkha mountains became a favorite place of meditation for Gelukpa practitioners. A century later the Second Dalai Lama's guru Norzang Gyatso made a fourteen year retreat here and attained enlightenment. The Second Dalai Lama came here frequently to meditate. In a poem he wrote,

Here I sit in the Jewel Snow Mountains,
Where meditation spontaneously achieves results....
Thoughts of my guru Khedrup Norzang Gyatso arise.
A flood of emotion surges up from within me,
And every hair on my body trembles with joy.

The region remains a hotbed of meditation even today, under Tibet's present difficult situation.

WORDS WRITTEN IN BLACK INK

ARE EASILY DESTROYED BY A DROPLET OF WATER;

BUT LOVE DRAWS A PICTURE ON THE HEART

THAT GOES DEEP AND ENDURES FOREVER.

■ FROM *SONG OF TANTRIC EXPERIENCE*

THE SIXTH DALAI LAMA, GYALWA TSANGYANG GYATSO

1683-1706

CHAPTER TEN

JHAMPA ZHISHI, TEMPLE OF THE RADIANT MAITREYA BUDDHA

NYONE VISITING LAMA TSONGKHAPA'S MEDITATION HERMITAGE at Olkha Cholung will want to visit the Maitreya Temple in the adjoining valley, known as Jhampa Zhishi. Here Tsongkhapa performed what is listed in his biography as one of his four greatest deeds: the restoration of the great Maitreya statue, and the temple in which it was housed. This "greatness" does not come from the physical size of the task, but from the mystical energies and prophecies surrounding Maitreya Buddha in general and the Jhampa Zhishi temple in particular.

As mentioned in an earlier chapter, in 838 A.D. Prince Lang Darma murdered his brother, King Tri Ralpachen (an early incarnation of the soul destined to become the Dalai Lamas), and stole the throne from him. He then went on to reverse the policies of his ancestors, and fiercely persecuted Buddhism. Monks and nuns were forced to disrobe, flee or die, and the temples and monasteries were left empty.

Many monks went into a self-imposed exile in the Tsongkha region of northeast Amdo (just east of Kokonor), where Tsongkhapa would be born five centuries later. In fact, Tsongkhapa's name means "The Man from Tsongkha." The three senior monks each planted a tree in Tsongkha and took an oath that, if the trees survived, they would take this as an omen that they should wait out the turmoil and then to return to Central Tibet to re-establish the monkhood. The trees (or at least offspring grown from them) still exist in Tsongkha (modern day Xining), and are objects of pilgrimage for Tibetans visiting the region.

The three monks indeed did return to Lhasa some years later, accompanied by two others, and initiated the process of rebuilding the Tibetan monkhood.

A number of new temples and monasteries also emerged at this time. The first of these was the Maitreya Temple near Olkha Cholung, known as the Jhampa Zhishi. It has the distinction of being the first temple to be built after the destruction and civil wars of the mid ninth century.

Maitreya Buddha was chosen as a symbol of this re-generation of Buddhism in Tibet, for Maitreya is the "Future Buddha" whose tradition, like that of Buddha Shakyamuni (and all one thousand universal teachers of this auspicious age), will last for 5,000 years.

Most Tibetan temples built prior to the creation of the Jhampa Zhishi Temple have a Shakyamuni statue as their main image. This changed from the time of the creation of the Jhampa Zhishi. From then until now, the trend has been much more toward having an image of Maitreya, the savior of the enlightenment tradition in the future. The Jhampa Zhishi Temple was an omen signaling this change.

When Tsongkhapa passed through the region in the late 1300s (almost four centuries after the creation of the Jhampa Zhishi), this temple had become abandoned and dilapidated. Tsongkhapa meditated in front of the sacred image, and fell into a state of vision. In the vision he was instructed to repair both the image and the temple, and that this would release a wave of enlightenment energy that would utterly transform Central Asia.

At the time he and his disciples were engaged in the practice known as "the twelve austerities," in which a practitioner must live by begging, is not allowed ever to own more than is required for one day of living, cannot sleep in a building that has both a roof and walls (i.e., can have one but not the other), can only wear clothing that has been discarded by others, and so forth.

Nonetheless they took it upon themselves to take up residence at the Jhampa Zhishi and restore it. They did this by begging for alms from pilgrims and travelers passing by, and working on the temple and images themselves. The project took almost two years, but eventually was successful. The group re-consecrated the Maitreya image, and that night Tsongkhapa dreamed that Maitreya Buddha sent forth a great blaze of light. The light covered the entire face of the earth and inspired all the living beings to evolve toward enlightenment.

Many years later, after Tsongkhapa had attained enlightenment and was in his old age, he built Ganden Monastery on Nomad Mountain as a seat for his lineages. "Ganden" is the Tibetan translation of the Sanskrit "Tushita," the name of the pure sphere associated with Maitreya Buddha. A large Maitreya statue adorned the main temple. In other words, his work of restoration of the Jhampa Zhishi Temple and the link with the Maitreya Buddha prophecies opened the karmic doors for the fulfillment of the destiny that was to follow. Ganden Monastery soon became the symbol of a movement that, within two centuries, became the largest school of Buddhism in Central Asia, and produced such illustrious luminaries as the Dalai Lamas and Panchen Lamas of Tibet, the Jetsun Dampa incarnations of Mongolia, the Bakula Rinpoches of Ladakh, and so forth.

Tsongkhapa's young disciple, the First Dalai Lama, similarly created a large Maitreya statue out of pure gold when he established Tashi Lhunpo Monastery forty years later. One night he had a dream similar to that of Lama Tsongkhapa, and the next day wrote a poem to Maitreya,

> When, like a sun rising from behind the mountains,
> The Buddha of Love appears at the Diamond Seat,
> May the lotus of wisdom be opened
> And living beings swarm to drink truth's honey....
>
> May all beings hold wisdom's handle,
> And fly the flag of spiritual learning that is
> Adorned by discipline, meditation and insight,
> That the banner of truth may everywhere be seen....

And through meditation upon Maitreya, the Buddha of Love,
May the living beings gain love's splendor
That dispels the shadow of evil,
And attain to the Great Illumination.

The Second Dalai Lama continued the Maitreya tradition when he created Gyal Monastery below the Oracle Lake, building a great Maitreya chapel and statue that outshone even these two earlier images.

The old pilgrimage route from Lhasa and Samye to the Oracle Lake passed through the small valley in which the Jhampa Zhishi Temple is located, and therefore was a very important power site in pre-Communist days. These days the motor road leaves it a bit off the beaten path.

The temple was badly damaged by the Communists in the 1960s, and its libraries were burned. The small quorum of monks living there received us graciously, and allowed us to meditate in the main assembly hall, in the presence of the holy Maitreya image.

JUST AS A REFLECTED IMAGE APPEARS

WHEN A MAN HOLDS HIS FACE IN FRONT OF A MIRROR,

AND THAT FACE SEEMS TO EXIST IN THE NATURE OF ITS APPEARANCE,

ALL THINGS APPEAR YET ARE OTHER THAN WHAT THEY SEEM.

THE FACE IN THE MIRROR IS NOT A PERSON, JUST A REFLECTED IMAGE.

YET FACE AND MIRROR MAKE THAT IMPRESSION.

FOR THAT SAME REASON, ALL THAT APPEARS FOLLOWS PHYSICAL LAW,

YET IS OTHER THAN WHAT IT SEEMS.

■ FROM *MEDITATIONS TO SEVER THE MIND FROM EGO*

THE SEVENTH DALAI LAMA, GYALWA KALZANG GYATSO

1708-1757

CHAPTER ELEVEN

TASHI LHUNPO AND TIBET'S "FATHER-SON" LEGACY

TWO ROADS RUN FROM LHASA TO SHIGATSE, where the First Dalai Lama built Tashi Lhunpo Monastery in 1447. The southern route passes the fabulous Turquoise Lake, or Yumtso, one of the highest lakes in the world. The road runs over two very high mountain passes, complete with glaciers. Local nomads often stand by the roadside by the glaciers, offering yak rides to pilgrims and tourists.

The other route lies to the north, and follows the river through the mountains. It passes by Yungdrung Ling, the principal Bon monastery in Central Tibet. Bon is often referred to in Western literature as "Tibet's pre-Buddhist religion." In fact it is a pre-Songtsen Gampo form of Buddhism, and these days resembles the other Buddhist schools in ninety percent of its training curriculum. Yungdrung Ling was destroyed by the Communists in the 1960s; but the mother of the former Panchen Lama was Bonpo, and so he personally raised the seed money for its restoration during the liberalization period of the 1980s.

The First Dalai Lama was born in the countryside of Tsang Province, of which Shigatse is the main town. As mentioned in the introduction, he was semi-orphaned at the age of seven, so his mother placed him in Nartang Monastery for both care and education. He quickly rose to become Nartang's most promising young monk scholar, and was given to the learned abbot for training. He was then sent to Lhasa when he was in his mid twenties, where he became a disciple of Lama Tsongkhapa just four years before the latter passed away. After Tsongkhaps'a passing he continued his training under Tsongkhapa's three principal disciples – Gyaltsepjey, Khedrupjey and Jey Sherab Gyatso — but became especially close to the third of these, Jey Sherab Gyatso, who was Tsongkhapa's main tantric disciple. The First Dalai Lama made numerous retreats under Jey Sherab Gyatso's supervision, and eventually attained realization.

The First Dalai Lama wrote many poems in praise of his main teachers. In the poem written to Tsongkhapa and his chief disciples he says,

> Above the peaks of the eastern snow mountains
> White clouds float high in the sky.
> There comes to me a vision of my teachers.
> Again and again am I reminded of their kindness;
> Again and again am I moved with emotion....

That I, Gendun Druppa, who tends to be lazy,
Now I have a mind somewhat propelled by Dharma,
Is due solely to the kindness of the incomparable
Tsongkhapa and his spiritual heirs.

Most excellent of spiritual guides, from now until
The essence of buddhahood is attained,
I need seek no other sources of guidance or inspiration.
Pull me to enlightenment's shores
With the hooks of your great compassion.

Tashi Lhunpo Monastery was created as a fruition of that aspiration, and was dedicated to the lineages that the First Dalai Lama had received from Lama Tsongkhapa and his chief disciples.

In reality the creation of Tashi Lhunpo was not the First Dalai Lama's personal wish, but came about because of the repeated requests of his patrons and disciples. From his side, for the past decades he had lived his life by spending half of his time in meditation retreat, and the other half as a travelling teacher, and this suited him very well. But then in the mid 1440s the spiritual and civic leaders of Tsang began to press him to create a monastery that would bring his enlightenment lineages to southwest Tibet. In addition, his senior students became concerned for his health, with all the travelling he was doing.

He accepted to consider the request, and made retreats in several places to observe for signs. During one of these retreats he received numerous visions, in which his guardian angel Palden Lhamo appeared to him and made a clear prophecy that he should create a monastery at the sky burial site near Shigatse. As he meditated, he heard Palden Lhamo pronounce the words "Tashi Lhunpo," or "Auspicious Mountain." He knew that this should be the name of the monastery.

As a result, he built Tashi Lhunpo Monastery directly on top of the sky burial site above Shigatse, with his own teaching throne immediately behind the rock on which bodies had been cut up in order to be offered to the birds. Anyone coming to him for blessings would have to stand on this rock and meditate on their own impermanence and death.

Many years later, when the young Second Dalai Lama was living in Tashi Lhunpo, he wrote a poem on the subject,

Whatever comes together one day must part;
At the end of every sowing comes the harvest
And then the process of recycling begins again.
This is the law of nature....
Therefore remember that life is fragile and quickly changes,

Like the weather in the midst of a lightning storm,
And make firm the powers of the spirit,
The only friend that is with you in every situation.
Enrich it with the inner jewels of the spiritual perfections:
Generosity, ethics, patience, enthusiasm, meditation and wisdom.

This passage expresses very succinctly what the First Dalai Lama wanted his disciples to think when they stood on the cutting rock in front of his throne in order to receive a hand blessing from him.

As mentioned in the previous chapter, the First Dalai Lama created a great Maitreya statue in Tashi Lhunpo, to continue the legacy of the Jhampa Zhishi Temple and of Tsongkhapa's visions at Ganden. The poem that he wrote on this occasion, and that I quoted in the previous chapter, is known by heart to most Tibetans.

When the First Dalai Lama was in his eighty-fourth year, he undertook a long teaching tour to all the major places where he had taught during his lifetime, and announced to his disciples that it would be his last visit with them. He passed away, seated in meditation, shortly after completing the tour and returning back to Tashi Lhunpo. The holy relics from his cremation pyre are still preserved in a small stupa in Tashi Lhunpo. On our visit, the monks graciously allowed us to meditate in this sacred chapel.

His reincarnation, the Second Dalai Lama, spent the first twenty years of his life in Tashi Lhunpo, but when he was in his early twenties he went to Central Tibet, and was received there with such enthusiasm that he was pressed to establish a seat in Drepung Monastery. This, as we saw when we visited Drepung near Lhasa, became the Ganden Podrang, and remained the principal seat of the Dalai Lamas from that time until after the Great Fifth became lama king of Tibet (an event that occurred in 1642) and moved the Dalai Lama residence to the Potala. Of course all Dalai Lamas would return to Tashi Lhunpo for a period in their lives, either in their youth to study or in their maturity to teach.

A few decades after the transition of the Dalai Lamas to Lhasa, a young monk was placed in Tashi Lhunpo for training. This was the reincarnation of the great Gyalwa Wensapa, one of the most spectacular and mystical characters in Tibet's history. After the Third Dalai Lama passed away and the Fourth was discovered, this lama became the Fourth's spiritual tutor; and when the Fourth died at a relatively young age, he also became tutor to the Great Fifth Dalai Lama. He was relatively old when the Great Fifth became lama king in 1642, and by that time had become the teacher of almost every Gelukpa monk and yogi in Central Asia. Among his disciples was the Jetsun Dampa of Mongolia, known today as Zanabazar (a Mongolian mispronunciation of the Sanskrit form of his Tibetan name, Yeshe Dorje, that in Sanskrit becomes Jnanavajra, i.e., Zanabazar). Zanabazar became lama king of Mongolia in the late 1680s, in a structure modeled after that used for the Dalai Lama Office in Tibet.

His great guru of both the Fifth Dalai Lama of Tibet and First Jetsun Dampa of Mongolia was known as Panchen Lozang Chokyi Gyaltsen, or Panchen Chogyen for short. Traditional Tibetan literature refers to him as the First Panchen Lama, although today three pre-incarnations are added to the list, so in Chinese literature he is always referred to as the Fourth Panchen.

After becoming lama king, the Great Fifth Dalai Lama requested his guru Panchen Chogyen to accept Tashi Lhunpo as his hereditary seat of reincarnation. This remained the case from that time onward. All future incarnations of the Panchen Lama were brought to Tashi Lhunpo Monastery for training, and made it their primary teaching seat. This continued until the destruction of the traditional Tibetan infrastructure by the Chinese in the 1960s and the imprisonment of the Panchen Lama in 1964.

From the time of this First Panchen Lama, the Panchen and Dalai Incarnations have been popularly known to Tibetans as *Yab Sey*, or "Father-Son." The idea is that whoever of the two is the older takes spiritual responsibility for the education and enlightenment of the other. Therefore whenever a Dalai Lama passes away, the search for and enthronement of his reincarnation is usually overseen by the Panchen Lama; and when a Panchen Lama dies, the Dalai Lama does the same for him. In addition, the older usually also becomes tutor to the younger, especially in the giving of monastic ordination, and also in the transmission of the tantric initiations and lineages.

For example, the present Dalai Lama was discovered with the help of the previous Panchen. There were three almost equally promising boys born in Amdo with auspicious signs; the Panchen was consulted (this was 1937 or 1938, I think), and recommended the boy who today is our Dalai Lama. Then after the previous Panchen died in 1989 (or was murdered by the Chinese, as is surmised by many Tibetans), the elders at Tashi Lhunpo Monastery secretly approached the Dalai Lama to oversee the search and for his reincarnation. (As readers familiar with modern Tibetan history will know, after announcements of the reincarnation was made by Dharamsala in 1995, the boy and his family were arrested, along with the head lama of Tashi Lhunpo and forty-eight of his monks, and an "alternate" Panchen candidate was enthroned. Amnesty International declared the boy the world's youngest political prisoner. He has not been seen since that time, and his whereabouts are not known today.)

The Panchen Lama was not able to escape into exile in 1959, when the Dalai Lama and a flood of other spiritual, cultural and civic leaders came to India. He attempted to work with the Chinese for several years to follow; but then in 1964 made a public speech stating the hopelessness of compromise. The following day he disappeared. He was presumed dead by the international community for the decade and a half to follow. Then after the death of Mao and the advent of liberalization, he once again emerged into public life. From then until his mysterious death a decade later, he worked tirelessly to rebuild Tibet's spiritual and cultural infrastructure, that had been so badly damaged during the radical Communist years. He began with the Jokhang in Lhasa, then expanded to the great monasteries and temples in Central Tibet, until there was nowhere in Tibet that his hand did not touch. In brief, he accomplished inside Tibet what the Dalai Lama has accomplished in the international arena.

The visit to Tashi Lhunpo stands as testimony to his great efforts. The monastery became badly damaged after his arrest in 1964, and the stupas holding the remains of his previous incarnations were destroyed, as were large sections of the monastery. Yet Tashi Lhunpo today has been restored to much of its former grandeur.

The Panchen Lamas continued the effort to fulfill the Maitreya prophecies, just as had Lama Tsongkhapa and the early Dalai Lamas. In 1914 the Sixth Panchen (Ninth by Chinese count) built an enormous Maitreya, eight-six feet in height, and with over six hundred pounds of gold in it. This was damaged by the Communists in the 1960s, but was restored by the Panchen Lama after his release from prison. It stands today as a testament to the Panchen Lama's commitment to spiritual and artistic excellence, and his visionary powers as a great spiritual leader.

People who make numerous pilgrimages to the great power sites develop special feelings for particular places in them. For me, my favorite in Tashi Lhunpo is the small chapel where the First Dalai Lama created a most wonderful state of the female buddha Tara. In addition to his talents as a teacher, writer and builder, he was also a good artist, and this small chapel houses several images that he fashioned with his own hand. When one sits there in meditation, one can almost feel the magical energies that were embodied in the lives and works of the early Dalai Lamas, and were continued later by the illustrious Panchen incarnations.

An air of sadness also pervades the halls of the monastery. The child who was recognized as the incarnation of the Panchen Lama in 1995 has disappeared, and even his photo is banned. Meanwhile, the alternate candidate that was enthroned is *persona non grata* with the Tibetans, who refer to him as *Gyami Panchen*, or "The Chinese Candidate, and also as *Panchen Zunma*, or "The False Panchen." He is rarely allowed to visit the monastery, and even then only with the tightest security that the Chinese can muster.

That said, the atmosphere on our visit was happy and auspicious. The very elderly Yondzin Rinpoche, tutor of the former Panchen Lama, was in residence. Now in his late eighties, he was giving a series of tantric initiations known as *Maitri Gyatsa*, or "The Hundred Lineages from (the Indian Mahasiddhas) Maitrepa." Thousands of monks and lay people were in attendance. We had the good fortune to sit outside the temple with the crowd for one of these cycles of initiation, and thus to receive the tantric blessings of Maitrepa from the great master who had tutored the Panchen Lama.

Turn the horse of the mind up the mountain path.

Control him with the reins of the three higher trainings

Of self-discipline, meditation and awareness.

Spur him on with the iron whip of joyful effort

And cut on to the open road to liberation.

■ from *Song of the Tantric Path*

The Seventh Dalai Lama, Gyalwa Kalzang Gyatso

1708-1757

CHAPTER TWELVE

METOKTANG AND GYAL MONASTERY

THE SECOND DALAI LAMA FIRST VISITED METOKTANG IN THE MID 1490S. At the time he was returning from a pilgrimage to Tsari, the sacred mountain in south Tibet that has one foot in Tibet, one in Bhutan and one in India. The king of Chonggyey sponsored the journey. Chongyey is famous in Tibet as the burial site of the early Tibetan kings of the Yarlung Dynasty. Later it would be the birthplace of the Fifth Dalai Lama.

The Second was a young man at the time, and took the opportunity to visit many of the places where disciples and patrons from his previous incarnation now lived. He wrote a wonderful epic poem, entitled *Song of the Travelling Bee*, describing the adventure. The poem opens with the following verse,

> There I was, living near Ehchok,
> Engaged in the pursuit of meditation
> On Shambo Mountain, a holy place
> Rivaling Mount Kailash itself in glory,
> When a powerful arrow of invitation arrived,
> Requesting me to come and teach.
> And I, a young monk well trained in Dharma,
> Jumped into the carriage of the wish to accept.

The poem goes on to describe his journey from Ehchok through Dvakpo, where Milarepa's disciple Gampopa had established a monastery that became the original seat of the Kargyu School. After much travel and many teaching events the group arrives at Tsari, where they make their circumambulation. They then begin the long return journey to Central Tibet.

However, on the way back the young monk experiences a dream of Metoktang, and has a distinct feeling that an important link to the fulfillment of his destiny lies there. He accepts an invitation to visit both Metoktang and the Oracle Lake above it.

He speaks of the visit in the following verse,

> On our journey back from Tsari,
> In order to see the great wilderness, and to behold
> Young peacocks dance and wild cuckoos sing,
> We travelled with some friends of good fortune
> To Metoktang, a place like no other,

Its earth clothed in every flower ornament.
We looked, and we delighted in
The playful expressions of goodness and joy.
Indeed, we painted the Odey Gungyal mountains there
With the dust from our pilgrimage footsteps.

The mountains behind Tsongkhapa's retreat hermitage at Olkha Cholung are known as the Odey Gungyal. The region was sacred to the ancient Tibetans, and became an important meditation region once Buddhism became the national religion. King Songtsen Gampo is said to have come here to meditate in the mid seventh century, as did the great Indo-Persian master Padma Sambhava, who oversaw the construction of Samye Monastery in the eighth century. While here Padma Sambhava performed tantric rituals in order to bind all of the traditional mountain and lake deities of the area to the protection of the Dharma.

Padma Sambhava is also said to have prophesied the Second Dalai Lama's work in the area, and his construction of the Gyal Monastery at Metoktang. The treasure text entitled A Guide to the Power Places of Yolmo states,

To the east of the Yolmo region
Is a place like a mound of jewels,
A secret site of great virtue....
I have buried 108 great treasures there....
Eh ma! This place that inspires joy
Is more radiant than any other.
It is a residence of Vajrasattva
And a place blessed by Avalokiteshvara.
The dakas and dakinis gather here,
And samadhi is accomplished without effort....
When the time comes to open the door to this holy place,
An emanation of Avalokiteshvara will appear,
A youth who carried the blessings of Vajrasattva,
Whom to see, hear or remember inspires great devotion.

Tibetans take the third to last line above to be the reference to the Second Dalai. The last line also gives the secret name for the Dalai Lama lineage, Tongwa Donden, or "He Meaningful to See." This is the name used for the Dalai Lama by the Nechung Oracle when the Oracle is in trance.

Atisha, whom we encountered in previous chapters, also prophesied the Second Dalai Lama's work at Metoktang and the building of Gyal Monastery. The prophesy appears in the eleventh century text known as the *Kadam Lekbam*, or *Book of the Kadampa Masters*. In it we read,

In the north, blessed by the presence of seven great kings (*gyalpo*)
Is a mandala-like plateau (*tang*), blue like lapis,
Adorned with walls like a thousand pearls,
A place blessed by a thousand buddhas (gyalwa).
It is adorned by a mountain shaped like a turquoise stupa,
And is the playground of a thousand dakinis,
A place most conducive for one-pointed meditation....
There a Victorious One (Gyalwa) will make his residence
And perform mystical activities to benefit the world....
Blessed by all the buddhas (gyalwa) of the ten directions,
It has a plateau (*tang*) as smooth as lapis luzuli
And is surrounded by a ring of majestic mountains....
It is adorned by numerous mystical signs
And is beautified by a net of radiant flowers (metok).

The repetition of the words Gyalpo, or king, and Gyalwa, or buddha (literally *jina* in Sanskrit) are taken as references to the Dalai Lama, who would become lama king of Tibet; and also to Gyal Monastery. Gyal was built on a plateau known as Metoktang, and again these syllables are repeated in the prophecy.

The passage, "There a Victorious One (Gyalwa) will make his residence / And perform mystical activities to benefit the world..." ... clearly refers to the Dalai Lamas, who are generally referred to as Gyalwa Rinpoche by all Tibetans. (Traditionally only Mongolians, Chinese and other foreigners use the name "Dalai Lama").

In many ways, the Second Dalai Lama's visit to the Oracle Lake, and his creation of the Gyal Monastery there, were instrumental to the success that all future Dalai Lamas would achieve. Every Dalai Lama since the Second (at least those who lived to maturity) visited and meditated here, and received visionary guidance in their life's work. Moreover, the Oracle Lake above Gyal Monastery would henceforth be used for divining the birthplaces of future Dalai Lama incarnations, as well as of many other incarnate lamas.

The Maitreya statue created by the Second at Gyal Monastery was legendary for its beauty and its artistic excellence. As we saw earlier, the First Dalai Lama created a similar Maitreya statue in Tashi Lhunpo several decades earlier. Panchen Yeshe Tsemo, a disciple of the First, was present at the consecrations of both Maitreya images: that in Tashi Lhunpo and that in Gyal. The Second Dalai Lama's biographer Yangpa Choje quotes Panchen Yeshe Tsemo as saying, "During the consecration of Jey Tamchey Khyenpa's (i.e. the First Dalai Lama's) Maitreya statue in Tashi Lhunpo, the skies were constantly filled with rainbows, flowers fell from space, and the earth shook many times. I thought that I would never again witness anything so overwhelmingly miraculous. However, the magical signs that occurred during the consecration of the golden Maitreya statue at Chokhor Gyal were even more amazing and fabulous...." He then goes on to describe the many auspicious signs that occurred.

Yangpa Choje also relates a dream that Panchen Yeshe Tsemo had that night. In the dream Maitreya Buddha sent out rays of light that shone on the earth, with each ray like a rope that touched each individual living being. The living beings grabbed the ropes, and by means of them pulled themselves up to enlightenment. This occurred in hundreds and hundreds of waves, with each subsequent wave representing a future generation of living beings.

Of course this sacred image was stolen by the Chinese Communists when they destroyed Gyal in the 1960s.

The Second Dalai Lama wrote numerous spiritual poems while living at Gyal. Similarly, the Third practiced meditation here on numerous occasions, and on several of these composed songs and poems. In one of them he writes,

> O yogis who strive with diligence
> In the meaningful wisdom yogas,
> To you I offer this melodious song
> Meant to sooth the ear that is agitated
> By the humdrum of mundane living.
>
> Glorious Metoktang, this site at which we have gathered,
> Has been blessed by the presence of
> Many accomplished masters of the past.
> It is beautified by a lake of lotus flowers
> And is an abode of the dakas and dakinis.
>
> Yes, the dakas and dakinis gather here
> Like clouds gathering in a winter sky,
> This sacred place where snow lies like a shawl
> On mountains that stretch up to the sky.
> As I sit in witness to this beauty,
> I cannot help but give voice to this song.
>
> In future generations, teachers and disciples alike
> Should come to this place of power
> To meditate, and to write on the holy Dharma.
> Would that not be an excellent response
> To this short song of mine?

We camped at Metoktang beside the ruins of Gyal Monastery for several days, making outings to the Oracle Lake for vision quests, just as the Third Dalai Lama had done when he wrote this song, and sat in meditation in what remained of the temples where the early Dalai Lamas had once sat.

In the inconceivable mansion of great bliss joyful to know

Sits the pure aspect of one's own body and mind as a god.

See this divinity in your own body, speech and mind.

Drop ordinary thinking, cultivate this extraordinary awareness of

the sacred.

Not allowing negative thoughts to arise, turn to the deep and

the radiant.

Cultivate unrelenting mindfulness, and hold it in the deep and

the radiant.

■ from *Song of the Four Mindfulnesses*

The Seventh Dalai Lama, Gyalwa Kalzang Gyatso

1708-1757

CHAPTER THIRTEEN

LHAMO LATSO, THE ORACLE LAKE

CENTRAL TIBET HAS FOUR SACRED LAKES, each of which is associated with a female protective deity. Presumably this legacy comes down from ancient pre-Buddhist times. But Buddhism tends to absorb the best of whatever exists in the traditions of the foreign lands where it finds itself. It does not regard this absorption as a corruption or distortion, but rather as practical evolution and integration.

Lhamo Latso is one of these four holy lakes, and in recent centuries the most important of them. All four have been important places of pilgrimage for Tibetans and other Central Asians for centuries, perhaps even millenniums, and remain as strong today as ever.

As mentioned in the previous chapter, King Songtsen Gampo is said to have come to meditate at the shores of the Lhamo Latso Lake in the seventh century, and Padma Sambhava in the eighth.

Padma Sambhava's visit was part of his tour of all the principal power places of Tibet that were associated with deities that had been worshipped in pre-Buddhist times. In each of the power sites he performed "binding rituals," which is a tantric term for sacred ceremonies that invoke the particular deities, and then extract an oath from them to serve as protectors of Dharma and the enlightenment tradition. His ritual at the Lhamo Latso Lake had the effect of changing the qualities of the energies emanating from the lake, and bringing them into harmony with the enlightenment tradition. Padma Sambhava did the same at all four sacred lakes of Central Tibet, as well as at many of the mountains and caves that had been used for meditation and spiritual practice by the Tibetans in the past.

Although Padma Sambhava's tantric work transformed the Lhamo Latso Lake into a more powerful place for Buddhist meditation practice and pilgrimage, it did not make it into an Oracle Lake. This task would await the coming of the Second Dalai Lama.

Padma Sambhava wrote, "This holy lake has given prophecies of seven great incarnations of Avalokiteshvara. The first's reincarnation (i.e., the Second Dalai Lama) will open and empower the lake. This in turn will empower 108 minor lakes." Thus the empowerment of the Lhamo Latso not only transformed its waters into an oracular vehicle for living beings, but also activated the spiritual energies of 108 other lakes in Central Asia.

In 1504 the Second Dalai Lama was invited by King Lhagyari Dzongpa (of present day Chusum, or "Three Rivers") to teach in the area. During that visit he received many invitations from the local civic leaders to build a monastery in Gyal. He writes in his *Autobiography*, "During that teaching tour, numerous people approached me with forceful requests to build a monastery at Gyal Metoktang. I did not have time to do so at the time, due to my other commitments; but their requests were an auspicious omen (for doing so later). Nonetheless I did lead a world purification rite at Gyal, in order to re-affirm my karmic connections with the place." Of note, the office of the Lhagyari Dzongpa king, who had sponsored the Second's visit, remained an important figure in Tibetan spiritual and civic history until the Chinese invasion of the 1950s.

Building work at Gyal began five years later, in 1509. The Second Dalai describes it as follows in his *Autobiography*, "The monastery seemed to rise up by itself. The construction materials, such as the stones, wood and clay, came forth quite magically.... It was as though we humans would build a little bit during the day, and then the spirits of goodness would slip in quietly at night and work until dawn.... The auspicious omens were amazing. Every day flowers fell from the sky, and rainbows hovered above us. At night we could hardly sleep because our minds were enthralled with so many auspicious dreams."

Two years later, in the summer of 1511, the Second Dalai Lama and his quorum of monks, disciples, patrons and builders were joined by three hundred highly accomplished lamas for a ten day prayer vigil. One night during this vigil the Second dreamed that a woman appeared to him, gave him a sword, and then said,

> Negative times are filled with waves of difficulties,
> And many hindrances arise at the path of enlightenment.
> Visions received from this lake can provide guidance and solutions,
> For the lake has the power of delivering paranormal visionary experience.

The sword proved to be the key to the opening of the oracular powers of the lake. During the previous summer, when the foundations for one of the temples of Gyal Monastery were being built, the work crew unearthed an ancient sword made of meteorite metal (*nam chak*). Everyone took this as an auspicious sign at the time, but did not see more in it. However, the Second Dalai Lama now understood the role of the sword in the mystical process of opening the lake.

His *Autobiography* tells a rather long story of how a black magician then stole the sword, and how he and his disciples to struggle to get it back. Eventually they succeeded (at least in regaining part of it), and performed the ritual for "opening the lake."

The Second describes the day in which the ceremony for opening the lake was performed. He writes, "When we arrived below the ridge overlooking the lake, a great clamor of sound arose from the skies, like that of a severe hailstorm. I had come with some ten ritual masters to open the gates of this sacred site.... We performed a rite of offering to the guardian spirits (from the ridge), and then went down to the shores of the lake. There we performed a ritual invocation of Palden Lhamo, and threw the sword into the waters."

He continues, "Suddenly the color of the lake began to transform before our eyes, becoming all colors of the rainbow one after the other. Numerous images began to appear in it, such as mandalas and so forth. Then it went as clear as the sky. After that, countless images appeared one after another from within the clarity …. Finally the lake seemed to bubble and boil, and to turn the color of milk. Not a drop of it appeared as mere water. During the entire period, the things seen in it were perceived by all simultaneously."

The Second Dalai Lama concludes by commenting, "Hundreds upon hundreds of people have visited the lake since that time in order to receive a vision from it…. For those of pure mind and aspiration, it has remained a mystical place of power able to inspire visionary experiences in an unbroken stream."

The Second Dalai Lama spent the remainder of his life moving between his residences of Drepung and Gyal Monastery, and of course continuing his teaching tours as well as his writing activities. The Lhamo Latso, however, always remained most close to his heart.

The geography of the viewing site is completely amazing, almost as though a giant divine hand scooped up a half mile of rocks and boulders, and dragged them up the hill to form a near perfect dam-like ridge.

The seat where the Second Dalai Lama performed the first part of his ritual in 1511 lies at the bottom of the ridge. All future Dalai Lamas visiting the lake have similarly sat here to perform their rituals and prayers. Pilgrims today begin the vision quest to the lake by circumambulating this throne – really just a coarse platform made from rock and clay – and then offer incense in a stone and clay cairn beside it.

One then climbs up to the ridge along a path that weaves its way around the boulders; and when one arrives at the top one sits perched on the ridge, looking down to the lake on the other side.

The ridge itself forms a solid line on the one side of the lake, with the valley of the lake forming a horseshoe-like shape. The lake, probably a few hundred meters below, first seems very far away, but as one gazes into it seems to become larger and closer. A ring of mountains surrounds the horseshoe valley on every side.

We sat there for several hours, surrounded by dozens of Tibetans who had similarly come on vision quests. As I mentioned in the introduction, eighteen of the twenty-one members of our pilgrimage had very strong experiences in their vision quests at the lake. One of our group, the jazz musician Steve Dancz, a normally very quiet and non-dramatic character, sat weeping on his rock like a baby, so overwhelming was his experience.

Metoktang and the Oracle Lake are rather high in the mountains, however, and the viewing ridge is something like 17,500 feet in altitude. After our vision quest was complete, we broke camp and retreated to lower climes. Our camp that night, now at a mere 13,500 feet, seemed almost like sea level in comparison.

Over the years after he opened and empowered the Lhamo Latso Lake, the Second Dalai composed numerous poems in praise of it. In one of these he wrote,

> For those who maintain the tantric precepts well,
> Visions of empty images and events
> Appear miraculously in its waters.
> There is nothing that cannot be seen in it....
> For those wishing enlightenment in one lifetime,
> It is a supreme place for meditation practice;
> All things appear in it in their infinity nature,
> And yet their finite, conventional presence is made obvious.
> This mystical lake thus points a yogi's mind
> To the sublime union of both infinity and the finite,
> The ultimate and conventional levels of being.

THE STARS, ORNAMENTS OF SPACE,

WITH ONE ANOTHER DO NOT RUN RACE.

BECAUSE OF THE EARTH'S ROTATION,

THEY SWING ACROSS THE HEAVENS.

LIKE THAT, THE MASTERS AND THE FORCES OF GOODNESS

OF AMBITION HAVE NO YEARNING;

IT IS IN ACCORDANCE WITH THE TRAINEE'S EVOLUTION

THAT THEY APPEAR AND LEAD THE WAY TO LIBERATION.

■ FROM *A SONG IN PAIRED VERSES*

THE SEVENTH DALAI LAMA, GYALWA KALZANG GYATSO

CHAPTER FOURTEEN

PROLOGUE

AFTER OUR VISION QUEST AT THE ORACLE LAKE WAS COMPLETE, we began the long drive southwest to Nepal.

The chapters as arranged in this book do not follow our actual pilgrimage route. I have arranged the narrative from the point of view of how best to tell the Dalai Lama story as the Tibetans see it, and as it encompasses the sacred sites that we visited. In fact after our arrival in Tibet we went to Lhasa rather than Tsetang and the Yarlung Valley, and visited the Lhasa power places first, including the Jokhang and its khorras, Drepung and Nechung, the Pabongkha and Sera walk, the caves at Drak Yerpa, and so forth.

After Lhasa we drove to the ferry crossing that carries pilgrims across the Yarlung Tsangpo to Samye Monastery, and made the walk up Chimpuk Mountain to the meditation caves of Padma Sambhava and his twenty-five accomplished disciples.

Mindroling lies on the south side of the riverbank on the road from Samye to Tsetang, and this was our next stop. We then spent several days in Tsetang, and visited the Yambhu Lagang and Dradruk Temples.

After that we drove to Olkha Cholung and Tsongkhapa's meditation caves; and while camped there made a day trip to Jhampa Zhishi. It was a two day ride from there to Metoktang, where we camped while making outings to the Oracle Lake.

The rest came later. A long day's ride took us back to Tsetang, and another long day's ride to Gyantse and Shigatse. After two nights in Shigatse we continued to Sakya for a night, and then to Tingri, below Mt. Everest. Part of the group made a side visit to the foot of the Everest North Face, to visit the caves there where Padma Sambhava and Yeshi Tsogyal had meditated, while the rest of us spent the time in Tingri. We then continued south to Nyelam and the Milarepa cave, and from there began the rapid descent from the high Tibetan plateau to the Friendship Bridge that connects Tibet with Nepal.

The Lhasa-Nepal road also has many spectacular views. Here I have not told the story of our pilgrimage as a group experience, but rather have told it from the perspective of the pilgrimage sites themselves, and of how these are linked to the Dalai Lama legacy. I wanted to objectify the experience and allow the photographs to carry the emotional texture of the adventure, rather than articulate this as non-fiction novelette. And I wanted to introduce the reader to the Dalai Lamas and their place in Tibetan history, rather than narrate the adventures and misadventures of a rag-tag group of Western Buddhists (and one incognito Bhutanese monk) meandering around the holy places of the Roof of the World.

The roads in Tibet have very much transformed since our pilgrimage to the Oracle Lake. China spent billions of dollars across all the territories under its control over the three years prior to the 2008 Olympics, especially on roads from the local airports to anywhere the authorities thought that foreign tourists might visit. Therefore the roads from the Gongkar airport to Lhasa and Tsetang, from Lhasa to Shigatse via the Turquoise Lake, and from Lhasa to Nepal, have radically transformed.

The opening of the train link from mainland China to Lhasa has brought in hundreds of thousands of new Han Chinese immigrants. China plans to extend these rail lines, with spider-like legs running up every valley inside Central Tibet. Given the efficiency of the dictatorial central planning system that is China today, and the harshness with which any argument, protest or resistance is met, we can safely predict that Tibet as it appears in this book will disappear within a decade or so. In the early 1960s the great American cultural explorer and writer made a documentary movie on Tibet, entitled *Requiem for a Faith*. A visit to Tibet today is a part of that requiem.

But one never knows. Tibetans regard pilgrimage as healing and transformative. The Chinese destroyed all but thirteen of the 6,500 Tibetan places of pilgrimage during the Communist Cultural Holocaust during the terrible period of the last fifteen years of Mao's life; but since the liberalization of the 1980s the Tibetans have rebuilt, at least to some extent, well over 1,000 of these. Tibetans believe that everything in life depends on energy and karmic unfoldment.

Perhaps the positive energy and good karma from peoples around the world visiting the sacred pilgrimage sites of Tibet and of the Dalai Lamas will bring about a happy ending to the saga. There are precedents in Tibetan history. The Mongols invaded Tibet in the 1200s, but ended up giving Tibet their independence in return for the lamas agreeing to serve as tutors to Mongolia's royal families. Lt. Col. Francis Younghusband invaded Tibet from British India in 1904; but while in Lhasa took a walk in the mountains and fell into a mystical trance. A year later the British withdrew from Tibet and gave it its independence. Younghusband returned to England and became the head of The Mystical Society, and donated much of the remainder of his life writing on spiritual subjects. There is no doubt that the Tibetan lamas enjoy a tremendous popularity throughout China today, especially with the younger and more educated Chinese.

It is not impossible that history could repeat itself.

CHAPTER FIFTEEN

THE CRYSTAL ROSARY

O UR PILGRIMAGE VISITED MANY OF THE POWER PLACES that were sacred to the early Dalai Lamas. We thought it appropriate to close with a translation of a long life prayer to the present Dalai Lama, who so well embodies and expresses the spiritual vision of these great incarnations.

I translated this text in the mid 1980s, some 25 years ago, with Ven. Doboom Tulku, who at the time was the private secretary to the Dalai Lama. The Dalai Lama was scheduled to give a Kalachakra empowerment to the Tibetan community in Switzerland, and the Swiss organizers wanted to publish his long life prayer for the event. The text came to Ven. Doboom's desk, and he asked me to help him prepare it.

The colophon to the Tibetan text gives the context in which it was originally written in 1939. The text says, " A prayer for the long life and success of Jey Tamchekhyenpa Kuntuzigpa Kundun Gyalwa Ngawang Lobsang Tenzin Gyatso Palzangpo (i.e., the Fourteenth Dalai Lama) was written by the Regent Reting Rinpoche for the young Dalai Lama's enthronement (of 1939)." All formal Tibetan texts referring to the present Dalai Lama use this long string of honorific names for him: Master All-Knowing, All-Seeing, Fully Present, Victorious Lord of Speech, He of Sublime Mind, Glorious Doctrine-Holder Ocean." The last bit, Doctrine-Holder Ocean, is a translation of his ordination name, Tenzin Gyatso. All Dalai Lamas from the Second until today have Gyatso as their last name, meaning Ocean or "Dalai." The text was chanted by thousands of monks at his enthronement in 1939, and daily by his closest devotees for several years to follow. Eventually it was replaced by a shorter version written by Kyabje Ling Dorjechang and Kyabje Trijang Dorjechang, respectively the senior and junior tutors of the Dalai Lama since the mid 1950s.

In some ways Reting Rinpoche's longer text is more interesting than the shorter and later one. It begins by making reference to many of the previous incarnations of the being who became the First Dalai Lama. In addition, it provides a more complete picture of the role the Dalai Lama plays in the Tibetan mind.

The use of Reting Rinpoche's text for the long life and success of the present Dalai Lama became politically incorrect after the Tibetan coup d'etat of 1947, in which the Dalai Lama's father was murdered, and shortly thereafter Reting Rinpoche was arrested, tortured and then killed in prison. The Lhasa aristocrats who were behind the coup held power in 1949, when Chairman Mao announced his intention to invade and colonize Tibet. Needless to say, they did not have the courage or integrity to organize any real resistance when the invasion came in 1951. Some of them later came into exile in India, when the Dalai Lama and other spiritual and civic leaders were forced to flee imprisonment or death. The others remained in Tibet as collaborators with the Chinese. Most are now dead.

Reting Rinpoche's text remained in the closet for three and a half decades, until the Tibetan community in Switzerland decided to resurrect it. I was honored to be half of the two-man team to translate it into English.

The text reveals the deep love that the Tibetans hold for the office of the Dalai Lama. Reting Rinpoche was the first guru of the present Dalai Lama, and thus was an extremely learned and spiritually accomplished spiritual master. His text also reveals all of the key points of the enlightenment tradition, from the three higher trainings of the Hinayana, the bodhisattva practices of the Mahayana, and the two yogic stages of the Vajrayana.

> In the sky of compassion's pure nature
> Appear clouds of unobstructed wisdom and mercy.
> They release a shower of immortality.
> The deities of longevity manifest
> And erect a pillar of undying diamond life.

> O most excellent lama, the radiance of your merit and wisdom
> Grew in strength for many aeons,
> And you overcame from within yourself
> The darkness of the two obscurations.
> As a result you now fill the world
> With the light of the twofold enlightened activities.

> In this way long ago you achieved full enlightenment
> In your life as the illustrious Buddha Kunpak,
> And thus now abide in the sphere of highest nirvana.
> Yet, moved by compassion, you manifest mysterious emanations
> Equal in number to the atoms of the world,
> Marvelous forms that are difficult for even
> The greatest of bodhisattvas to comprehend.

> You manifested a pearl necklace of incarnations in India
> In order to illuminate the vast and profound ways of Dharma.
> Marvelous indeed was your string of lives
> As realized yogis accomplished masters and world leaders,
> Such as the Brahmin boy Keyu Nangwa.

> Deeply moved by sympathy for all living beings,
> You lived the legacy of universal love
> And manifested the bodhisattva deeds that deliver
> A feast of supreme and peerless joy
> To countless living beings.

Then in order to fulfill the wishes of the buddhas,
You accepted to incarnate here in Tibet,
This northern land covered in snow,
 And as a line of kings who illuminated
The land's affaires both mundane and supreme.

King Nyatri Tsanpo, King Tori Nyanshal
And the Buddhist patrons King Songtsen Gampo,
King Trisong Deutsen and King Tri Ralpachen:
These are a few of your royal incarnations.

After this you incarnated as numerous Tibetan masters,
Including the illustrious master Lama Drom Tonpa,
The accomplished sage Lama Nyanral Nyima Oser,
And Guru Chowang, revealer of treasure texts.

Then for four incarnations (as the first four Dalai Lamas),
From Gendun Drub to Yonten Gyatso,
Who were skilled in pouring forth the nectars
Of Lama Tsongkhapa's legacy upon fortunate trainees,
You strove to preserve the essential wisdom doctrines.

After this as the great Fifth Dalai Lama,
Gyalwa Ngawang Lobzang Gyatso,
Who was blessed by Manjushri the Bodhisattva of Wisdom,
You stood like Mt. Meru, the king of mountains,
In the center of the continents of masters and yogis,
And embodied the compassion of an ocean of buddhas
Possessing the highest and most sublime of wisdoms.

Then from the time of the Sixth Dalai Lama-
Gyalwa Tsangyang Gyatso, a master who was most wise
In teaching the ocean of Dharma
By means of beautiful poetry and song
In accord with the inclinations of trainees-
Until the Great Thirteenth, Gyalwa Tubten Gyatso,
Who was an ocean-like holder of Buddhist lineages-
You took birth repeatedly as a bodhisattva
And performed countless mysterious deeds.

Yet even now you continue to exert yourself and strive

To dispel darkness from within Tibet,
And have again sent forth a marvelous emanation,
This illustrious (Fourteenth Dalai Lama) incarnation,
A rising sun ablaze with the radiance of compassion
To simultaneously illuminate a hundred thousand lineages
In the lotus garden of the enlightenment lore.

O master equal to the Wisdom Bodhisattva,
Whose sublime wisdom, deep as ocean,
Upholds the legacy of the buddhas,
O lord over three worlds, matrix of all peerless qualities,
I offer this prayer to you.

You who reside in the heart of the Wisdom Bodhisattva,
May you become an ocean of wisdom into which
All the sutra and tantra lineages collect.
May you then remain with us forever, and
Work to preserve the ocean of teachings
With your sublime wisdom and unequaled skill.

Crown jewel of all the three worlds,
Remain with us forever to increase
The light of prosperity and joy
By making shine the sun and moon
Of your spiritual and temporal leadership.
Fill the skies of the four directions
With the brilliance of enlightenment lore.
Remain until the end of time
As protector of this Land of Snows.
Continue to incarnate until all beings are enlightened,
Emanating the mysterious deeds of body, speech and mind,
And bestowing blessings of the four excellences:
Spiritual knowledge, prosperity, happiness and freedom.

Remain with us untiringly;
And make manifest the realm of the three liberations,
The sphere in which samsara and nirvana are the same,
Radiate forth a hundred thousand lights
From the sun and moon of your great bliss

To guide all living beings through the paths and stages
Of spiritual growth leading to freedom and joy.

A diamond body of incomparable wonder manifests
From the ocean of compassion of all the buddhas,
A magnificent jewel of three mysteries
Resting amidst the four splendors.
O incomparable one, remain firmly with us forever.

Although you are absorbed in the formless wisdom
Of emptiness free from all distinctions,
Nonetheless you have manifested in this body
That is visible to trainees of good fortune.
O venerable lama, I request you,
Stay with us and illuminate the way.

O spiritual friend fulfilling the hopes
Of an ocean of living beings,
Remain as firmly as the great king of trees,
Your branches spread wide with knowledge, mercy and power,
And heavily laden with the fruits of the three enlightenment kayas.

One grows in freedom merely on seeing
Your holy body with the 112 marks and signs of perfection,
Or hearing your holy voice so beautifully melodious
With the sixty qualities of excellence,
Or recollecting your mind, with its wisdom
Of the non-duality of being and non-being.
O Master, remain with us forever,
The forces supporting you always firm.

O Excellent One, remain with us
And fulfill the wishes of beings without number.
Become a wish-fulfilling tree that stands on the root
Of having gathered 100,000 teachings,
Of having deeply contemplated their essence,
Like leaves of a tree rustling in the wind,
And of having become spiritually mature through meditation
Upon the coarse and subtle twofold path,
Like a tree with its branches heavily laden with fruit.

O Holy One, eye of the world,
May you remain with us forever
And fulfill the three legacies of a master:
Giving spiritual teachings that reveal
The essential thought of the buddhas;
Leading discussions that dispel mistaken dogmas;
And composing texts that fill with delight
The fortunate beings that love profound realizations.

Remain with us forever
As a great navigator of living beings.
Fulfill ordinary and higher aims of living beings
By sailing the ship of profound learning
In the traditions of the sutras and tantras,
Your driving force the strong and steady wind
Of the three noble disciplines.

O you who are the embodiment
Of the three great bodhisattvas--
Manjushri, whose nature is knowledge of emptiness,
Avalokiteshvara, who watches mercifully over the world,
And Vajrapani, lord of the secret way,
The bodhisattva of unsurpassed power
Able to crush the armies of evil--
O excellent one, remain with us forever.

Remain with us forever,
As a great protector of life,
Your body exquisite like a lotus,
Your speech as melodious as the music
Created by the gods of song,
And your mind clearly seeing
All aspects of reality.

Remain with us forever,
Roaming on the snow mountain of perfect ethics,
Shaking the mane of your magnificently bold samadhi,
And roaring like a lion with the wisdom
That devours the corpse of ignorance.

O Protector of the Land of Snows,
Which these days is steeped in darkness,
Remain with us unwaveringly,
Even until the end of the world.
Let blaze the light of your compassion
And fill this world with peace and joy.
Make firm the seven spiritual qualities within yourself
And take your seat on Dharma's golden throne,
Which is engraved with symbols of immutable wheels
And supported by eight fearless lions of enlightenment.
Do not allow the wisdom tradition to wane,
And instead strive hard to increase it in glory.

You have returned to us from [Amdo, in] the east,
Like the sun, friend of the flowers,
Possessor of eight divine qualities,
Rising from behind the eastern mountains,
Home of the greatest of gods.
O Supreme One, release a hundred lights
Of enlightened activities that will overpower
The corruptions that darken this world.

May the root of your great compassion
Remain always firm without any weakness;
May you stretch out a thousand limbs
Of the ten noble disciplines;
And may you refresh all the living beings
In the cool shade of your perfect joy.

May you tame the arrogant beings
Who are most difficult to tame
By means of turning ten times
The great wheel of the four trainings,
Thus bringing them to true spiritual knowledge
And releasing a celebration of wisdom and joy.

May you lift up your vajra might
And release the thunder of glory
Which crushes to powder all harmful forces
And negative energies that obstruct the world's joy.

May your throne, which possesses the four splendors
And symbolizes your spiritual and secular leadership,
Be ever rich with a hundred supreme joys.
May the summer lake of the Ganden Podrang ever thrive,
And may you meet with every excellent success.

May the pillars supporting the edifice of your life
Constantly stand as undying vajra elements,
That through the force of good karma you may carry
The banner of enlightened activity
As a supreme leader among gods and men
To the very peak of the world.

May those who train under you never be obstructed
In spiritual study, contemplation and meditation,
That they may rapidly and easily cross the twofold path
Of the quick and joyous tantric way,
Gaining spiritual powers both mundane and supreme.
May those who assist you and carry out your work
Have the wisdom to implement your wishes skillfully,
And to lead your people in glory
Of the Dharma's waxing moon.

May you be a constant rainfall flowing without partiality
To preserve the teachings and the practices
Of the enlightenment tradition in general and also
The lineage of the Second Buddha Tsongkhapa,
That these may never weaken or disappear.

May the holders of the various enlightenment lineages
Be adorned with the canopy of the three ways of a sage
And have the strength to hold on high the gem
Of the four ways of benefiting fortunate trainees.
May they enhance the surging currents
Of the river of enlightenment transmission

May the Sangha, embodiment of the seven noble jewels,
Live in harmony and with pure ways.
May they follow the paths of study, contemplation and meditation,
And engage in the activities of teaching, inquiry and composition,

So that they might fulfill every Dharmic legacy
And the enlightenment tradition may remain strong.

May the cold winter of violent ways
Subside throughout the world,
Especially in Tibet, Mongolia and China;
That the goodness and joy of the queen of spring may come,
And the summer face of enlightenment be revealed within our minds.

May enlightened thoughts and deeds,
Forces that eliminate obstacles to prosperity and joy,
Cause every force of evil to be calmed
And to lose its power to harm,
Such as the destructive attacks on religious freedom
Made by barbarians and evil spirits today.

O Great Guru, Holder of the White Lotus,
May you continue to manifest as a teacher of the Great Way
Until all living beings crossed the paths and stages
That lead to great enlightenment,
And the two purposes are spontaneously fulfilled.

May the mighty Dharma Protectors,
With whom you have long been familiar, such as
Palden Lhamo, Bektsey Chamdrel, Gyalchen Ku Nga
And especially the sworn one Dorjey Drakden (i.e., the Nechung Oracle),
Release an immediate force of the four magical activities.

By the strength of the blessings of the unfailing Refuge Jewels,
The power of the truth of the unchanging ultimate sphere,
And the mighty current of universal love,
May all themes of this prayer be auspiciously accomplished
Spontaneously and without the slightest hindrance.

OTHER BOOKS BY GLENN H. MULLIN

The Tibetan Book of the Dead: An Illustrated Edition, with photos by Thomas Kelly, Roli Books, New Delhi, 2009

Buddha in Paradise: A Celebration in Himalayan Art, Rubin Museum of Art, NY, 2007

The Flying Mystics in Tibetan Buddhist Art, Serindia Publications, Chicago and London, 2006

The Second Dalai Lama: His Life and Teachings, Snow Lion Publications, Ithaca, NY, 2005

Living in the Face of Death, Snow Lion Publications, Ithaca, NY, 2004

The Female Buddhas : Women of Enlightenment in Tibetan Mystical Art, Clear Light Publications, Santa Fe, 2003

The Fourteen Dalai Lamas: A Sacred Legacy of Reincarnation, Clear Light Publications, Santa Fe, 2001

Gems of Wisdom from the Seventh Dalai Lama, Snow Lion Publications, Ithaca, NY, 1999

Readings on the Six Yogas of Naropa, Snow Lion Publications, Ithaca, NY, 1998

Tsongkhapa's Six Yogas of Naropa, Snow Lion Publications, Ithaca, NY, 1997

The Mystical Arts of Tibet, Longstreet Press, Atlanta, 1996

The Dalai Lamas on Tantra, Snow Lion Publications, Ithaca, 1995

Mystical Verses of a Mad Dalai Lama, Quest Books, Chicago, 1994

Training the Mind in the Great Way: A Commentary by the First Dalai Lama, Snow Lion Publications, Ithaca, NY, 1993

The Practice of Kalachakra, Snow Lion Publications, Ithaca, NY, 1991

The Art of Compassion, Tibet House, New Delhi, 1989

Selected Works of the Thirteenth Dalai Lama: Path of the Bodhisattva Warrior, Snow Lion Publications, Ithaca, NY, 1988

Selected Works of the Sixth Dalai Lama: Songs of Love and Laughter, Tushita Books, Dharamsala, India, 1987

Death and Dying : The Tibetan Tradition, Penguin Arcana, London, 1986

Selected Works of the Second Dalai Lama: The Tantric Yogas of Sister Niguma, Snow Lion Publications, Ithaca, NY,1985

Meditations on the Lower Tantras: Translated Works by the Early Dalai Lamas, Library of Tibetan Works and Archives,Dharamsala, India, 1984

Selected Works of the Third Dalai Lama: Essence of Refined Gold, Snow Lion Publications, Ithaca, NY,1983

Selected Works of the First Dalai Lama: Bridging the Sutras and Tantras, Snow Lion Publications, Ithaca, NY,, 1982

Selected Works of the Seventh Dalai Lama: Songs of Spiritual Change, Snow Lion Publications, Ithaca, NY, 1981

Six Texts Related to the Tara Tantra, from the Works of the First Dalai Lama, Tibet House, New Delhi, 1980

Atisha and Buddhism in Tibet, Tibet House, New Delhi, 1979

The Practice of Vajrabhairava, Tushita Books, India, 1979

Lama Mipam's Commentary to Nagarjuna's Stanzas for a Novice Monk, Library of Tibetan Works and Archives, Dharamsala, India, 1978

Four Songs to Jey Rinpoche, Library of Tibetan Works

ABOUT THE AUTHOR

GLENN H. MULLIN is a Tibetologist, Buddhist writer, translator of classical Tibetan literature, and teacher of Tantric Buddhist meditation. He divides his time between writing, teaching, meditating, and leading tour groups to the power places of Nepal and Tibet.

Glenn lived in the Indian Himalayas between 1972 and 1984, where he studied philosophy, literature, meditation, yoga, and the enlightenment culture under thirty-five of the greatest living masters of the four schools of Tibetan Buddhism.

Glenn is the author of over 20 books on Tibetan Buddhism. He has also worked as a field specialist on three Tibet-related films and five television documentaries, and has co-produced five audio recordings of Tibetan sacred music. In 2002 his book The Fourteen Dalai Lamas was nominated for the prestigious NAPRA award for best book, and in 2004 his book The Female Buddhas won a Best Book Award from Foreword Magazine.

After returning from India in 1984 Glenn founded and directed The Mystical Arts of Tibet, an association of Dharma friends that was instrumental in bringing the first tours of Tibetan monks to North America to perform sacred Temple music and dance, as well as create mandala sand paintings. He gave this to Drepung Loseling Monastery in 1994, and it continues to bring Tibetan spiritual culture on tours around the world.

As well as leading tour groups to the Buddhist power places of Nepal and Tibet, Glenn acts as consultant and advisor to independent groups wanting to travel safely and meaningfully through these sacred sites.

http://www.glennmullin.com/new/index.php

ABOUT THE PHOTOGRAPHERS

Gerry Croce is the proprietor of Co-Logic Software Inc., which enables him to satisfy his interest in travel and to explore Asian culture and philosophy. In particular, through contact with the Tibetan people he has developed a deep appreciation for the Buddhist way of life.

Steve Dancz narrates and composed music for the film "The Sacred Sites of the Dalai Lamas" as well as numerous scores for National Geographic Films, including the PBS Special "Inside Mecca." He has performed at the World Festival of Sacred Music (India) at the request of His Holiness, the XIV Dalai Lama.

Rob Deming has had a lifelong interest in guitars, motorcycles, meditation, philosophy and computers and continues to struggle to differentiate them. He aspires to live by the quote "The price of freedom is everything," but is far too comfortable to act.

Michael Wiese is a filmmaker and a publisher of filmmaking and spiritual books. His recent films include the companion film to this book, "The Sacred Sites of the Dalai Lamas," "The Shaman and Ayahuasca" (Peru), and "Talking With Spirits" (Bali). He is currently editing a film of Lama Chime Rinpoche.

William P. Wood Jr. is a software engineer living in Villanova, Pa. After majoring in computer science at the University of Pennsylvania, he has worked at GlaxoSmithKline since 1983. A regular meditator for many years, he jumped at the chance to accompany Glenn Mullin on a vision quest to Tibet.

ABOUT THE EDITOR

Donald McCrea is a San Francisco songwriter and photographer. He edited the acclaimed photography book, "Migration" which was selected by American Photography Magazine as one of the Top Ten Photography books of 2010. Over the past thirty years he has done fashion and product photography.

Michael Wiese with Drepung monks

Steve Dancz with Samye pilgrims

IMAGE TITLES AND CREDITS

copyright page: Glenn H. Mullin, Kumbum Stupa. Gyantse / Michael Wiese

candle: Drepung Monastery / Rob Deming

ferry crossing the Brahmaputra River, Samye / Michael Wiese

2 Potala Palace / Rob Deming

3 Potala Palace from the roof of The Jokhang / Rob Deming

4 Sakya / Gerry Croce

5 Potala Palace / Gerry Croce

6 Kathmandu / William P. Wood Jr.

7 Lhasa / Michael Wiese

8 Boudhanath, Katmandu / Rob Deming

9 Nechung Monastery / Rob Deming

10 Patan Durbar Square, Kathmandu / William P. Wood Jr.

11 Jokhang Temple / Rob Deming

12 Kumbum Stupa, Gyantse / Michael Wiese

13 Barkhor Square, Lhasa / William P. Wood Jr.

14 Potala Palace / Rob Deming

15 Potala Palace / Rob Deming

16 Drepung Monastery / Rob Deming

17 Jokhang Temple / William P. Wood Jr.

18 Jokhang Temple / William P. Wood Jr.

19 Jokhang Temple / William P. Wood Jr.

20 Drepung Monastery / William P. Wood Jr.

21 Mindrolling Monastery / William P. Wood Jr.

22 Patan Museum, Kathmandu / William P. Wood Jr.

23 Kangyur Stupa / Rob Deming

24 Sangtsen Gampo Caves Rob Deming

25 Jokhang Temple / William P. Wood Jr.

26 Rongbuk Monastery, Mt Everest / William P. Wood Jr.

27 Drepung Monastery / Gerry Croce

28 Potala Palace / Rob Deming

29 Potala Palace / Rob Deming

30 Drepung Monastery / William P. Wood Jr.

31 Lambhu Lagang / Steve Dancz

32 Drepung Monastery / William P. Wood Jr.

33 Drepung Monastery / William P. Wood Jr.

34 Drepung Monastery / Rob Deming

35 Drepung Monastery / Steve Dancz

36 Jokhang Temple / William P. Wood Jr.

37 Drepung Monastery / Rob Deming

38 Drepung Monastery / Rob Deming

39 Nechung Monastery / Rob Deming

40 Nechung Monastery / Steve Dancz

41 Kangyur Stupa / Rob Deming

42 Kangyur Stupa / Rob Deming

43 Nechung Monastery / Steve Dancz

44 Drak Yurpa / Steve Dancz

45 Drak Yerpa Caves / William P. Wood Jr.

46 Sangtsen Gampo Caves / Rob Deming

47 Zhangmu, border of Tibet and Nepal / William P. Wood Jr.

48 Gyatse / Gerry Croce

49 Rongbuk Monastery, Mt Everest / William P. Wood Jr.

50 Sangtsen Gampo Caves / Rob Deming

51 Drak Yurpa / Gerry Croce

MW an imprint of MICHAEL WIESE PRODUCTIONS

DIVINE
ARTS

DIVINE ARTS sprang to life fully formed as an intention to bring spiritual practice into daily living. Human beings are far more than the one-dimensional creatures perceived by most of humanity and held static in consensus reality. There is a deep and vast body of knowledge — both ancient and emerging — that informs and gives us the understanding, through direct experience, that we are magnificent creatures occupying many dimensions with untold powers and connectedness to all that is. Divine Arts books and films explore these realms, powers and teachings through inspiring, informative and empowering works by pioneers, artists and great teachers from all the wisdom traditions.

We invite your participation and look forward to learning how we may better serve you.

Onward and upward,

Michael Wiese
Publisher/Filmmaker

DivineArtsMedia.com

OUR FILMS

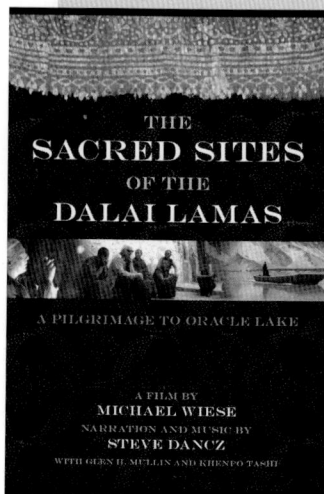

THE SACRED SITES OF THE DALAI LAMAS
A PILGRIMAGE TO THE ORACLE LAKE

A FILM BY MICHAEL WIESE

NARRATION AND MUSIC BY
STEVE DANCZ

OFFICIAL
SELECTION
ATLANTA
FILM FESTIVAL

This remarkable film visits the sacred sites of the Dalai Lamas in Tibet, tracing a pilgrimage with translator and author Glenn Mullin. This fascinating journey explores the caves where the early Buddhist masters meditated, enters the monasteries where the Dalai Lamas and others taught, and — at an altitude of over 16,000 feet — looks down into the famous oracle lake of Lhamo Lhatso (where every Dalai Lama has had prophetic visions).

The sacred sites:
Potala · Jokhang · Drepung Monastery · Nechung · Drak Yerpa Valley · The caves of Songsten Gampo, Jowo Atisha, and Guru Rinpoche · Samye Monastery · Lambhu Lagang Castle · Ani Sanku Nunnery · Lama Tsongkhapa Meditation Cave · Tranduk · Kangyur Stupa · Terdak Lingpa · Tashi Lumpo · Champa Zhishi · Sakya · Chokhor Gyal · Milarepa's Cave · The Oracle Lake

"... a rare film. Wiese has created a work of art that focuses on the country of Tibet and the amazing resilience of the Tibetans... a 'must see' film for anyone interested in Buddhism, Tibet, or Tibetan culture."
   — Elephant Journal

"Sacred Sites is visually rich, with footage of an incredible variety of Buddhist sites. While its sprawling outdoor shots of mountains and valleys are gorgeous, the real beauty of this documentary is in how it captures ordinary people in their environments....offers a glimpse of things so rarely seen."
   — Tricycle Magazine

Special features include two 20 minute segments, *The Art of Pilgrimage* with Glenn Mullin and *A Monk's Perspective* with Khenpo Tashi.

DVD ALL REGIONS $24.95 | ORDER NUMBER: TIBET | ISBN: 1932907211 | 2 HOURS
1.800.833.5738 · 25% DISCOUNT AVAILABLE ONLINE AT WWW.DIVINEARTSMEDIA.COM